A Funny Thing Happened
on the Way to the School Library

A Funny Thing Happened
on the Way to the School Library

A Treasury of Anecdotes, Quotes, and Other Happenings

LARRY A. PARSONS

Illustrated by
Janet Askew
and
Kathleen Spradlin

1990
LIBRARIES UNLIMITED, INC.
Englewood, Colorado

LIBRARIES UNLIMITED, INC.
P.O. Box 3988
Englewood, CO 80155-3988

Library of Congress Cataloging-in-Publication Data

Parsons, Larry A.
    A funny thing happened on the way to the school library : a treasury of anecdotes, quotes, and other happenings / Larry A. Parsons.
        xix, 204 p. 22x28 cm.
        Includes bibliographical references.
        ISBN 0-87287-751-5; 90 -42344
        1. School libraries--Anecdotes. 2. Library science--Anecdotes.
    3. School libraries--Humor. 4. Library science--Humor.
    5. Librarians--Anecdotes. 6. Librarians--Humor. I. Title.
    Z675.S3P237   1990
PRO 020'.207--dc20   90-42344
    PAR   CIP

For Nancy Motomatsu for all the help she has so unselfishly given to librarians and other educators, and for being a friend.

Contents

Part 1 — Librarians

Part 2 — Free People — Free Libraries

Part 3 — Technology in the Library

Part 4 — The School and Community

Part 5—Kid Stuff

Part 6—Library Media Essays

Part 7—Potpourri

Preface

In this book, I have tried to take an eclectic look at those things (books, reading, children, technology, schools, administrators, etc.) which make up a school librarian's life. In so doing I hope to share some laughs, stories, and perhaps even an insight or two with kindred spirits.

Peggy Agostino Sharp was the first person I heard adequately define my job when she said, "A library media specialist is an identity crisis waiting to happen."

Our identity crisis is so severe that we cannot even agree on what we should call ourselves! Some of the more popular things we have been called are librarians, library media specialists, media specialists, learning resource specialists, instructional media specialists, and information specialists. We work in places with names just as varied. Regardless of what title rolls out next, folks back home will call us librarians, and we will always work in the library. Please forgive me if I, and the wonderful people who have sent material for this book, use our various titles and names interchangeably.

The library media specialist's identity crisis seems to stem from the fact that he or she strives to be a proactive supplier of information and services to a schizoid institution—American education. Educational institutions may not know where they are going, but library media specialists are expected to instantly provide information for it from an exploding universe of data, while still providing the same services as yesteryear, usually at reduced budgetary levels.

Countless educators have been contacted in order to gather information for this book. I sincerely thank everyone who took time from hectic schedules to respond. It was evident that the teachers, librarians, and administrators who responded were certainly caring, insightful folks. If we are indeed a "nation at risk," it is not for lack of intelligent, committed individuals. Perhaps we just need a dose of vision and leadership. The time is ripe for the second coming of Carnegie.

I especially want to express my sincere thanks to Janet Askew for her numerous cartoons and artwork, and to Mandy and Kevin Askew for all the help that they gave their mother. I am also grateful to Kathleen Spradlin (and her daughter, Mandy) for her cartoons. The representation of the school lockers was created by Jason Morgan on W. F. West High School's (Chehalis, Washington) Macintosh computers. The Computer Ball drawing was done by Edward Pun. The Washington State Coalition Against Censorship provided the cartoons dealing with censorship. I am responsible for the rest of the computer artwork, with help from Libraries Unlimited's *Print Shop Graphics for Libraries*.

Scores of people volunteered so much of their time and talent, I am sorry that I could not use everything submitted.

Grateful acknowledgment goes to the *U*N*A*B*A*S*H*E*D Librarian* and Carol Hole for allowing me to adapt her "Hardnox University." I also wish to acknowledge and thank the following for permission to use copyrighted material: Simon & Schuster, *Emergency Librarian*, *Connecticut Libraries*, ABC-CLIO, and *Wilson Library Bulletin*.

Special thanks is owed to Margie Thomas and Lawrence L. Jaffe, not only for their contributions, but for spreading the word in their various parts of the country. I appreciate the helpful blurbs in *Voice of Youth Advocates*, *The Book Report*, *School Library Media Quarterly*, *Education Week*, and various state publications.

It has been great fun gathering the items for this book. I hope you will find it enjoyable, too.

Contributors

Carlene M. Aborn
Osceola High School
Seminole, Florida

Judith Alexander
Mountlake Terrace Elementary School
Seattle, Washington

Eileen Andersen
Sehome High School
Bellingham, Washington

Florence Anrud
Iva Alice Mann Junior High
Tacoma, Washington

Sue Ardington
W. F. West High School
Chehalis, Washington

Janet Askew
Breidalblik Elementary
Poulsbo, Washington

Cathy Baker
Batavia High School
Batavia, Ohio

Elizabeth Beckman
Hayward Middle School
Hayward, Wisconsin

Erma V. Berkley
Port Angeles High School
Port Angeles, Washington

Anne Betts
Philipsburg Junior High School
Philipsburg, Pennsylvania

Pat Bowers
Hallinan Elementary School
Lake Oswego, Oregon

Carol Braden
Regina High School
South Euclid, Ohio

Linda Brake
Evergreen High School
Vancouver, Washington

Barbara Brehm
Urbana, Illinois

Bobbie L. Brooke
McElwain Elementary School
Denver, Colorado

Betty Jo Buckingham
Department of Education
Des Moines, Iowa

Cheryl Budgett
Jefferson-Lincoln Elementary School
Centralia, Washington

Marianne Candioglos
Franklin Elementary
Tacoma, Washington

Judy Carlson
Nisqually Middle School
Olympia, Washington

Bev Carlson
Sunset View Elementary School
Kennewick, Washington

Jo Chinn
Sequim Middle School
Sequim, Washington

Pamela L. Christian
Alumna
Fullerton Union High School
Fullerton, California

Ellen Clayton
The Indianola Academy
Indianola, Mississippi

Irene Clise
Timberline High School
Lacey, Washington

Candy Colborn
Cherry Creek Elementary
Englewood, Colorado

Deborah M. Cooke
Salem Church Middle School
Richmond, Virginia

Jane Cribbs
Lordstown Elementary School
Warren, Ohio

Paula D'Ambrosio
Stevenson High School
Sterling Heights, Michigan

Doris Dale
Southern Illinois University
Carbondale, Illinois

Renee Domogauer
Broadneck Senior High School
Annapolis, Maryland

Don Dresp
Thomas Branigan Memorial Library
Las Cruces, New Mexico

Mary Driver
Crump Elementary School
Memphis, Tennessee

Helen Fagan
Cornersville High School
Cornersville, Tennessee

Anne Filson
Forestville Elementary School
Great Falls, Virginia

Bettie T. Furrie
Follett Software Company
Chicago, Illinois

Robert G. Gabrio
Auburn, Washington

Eric Garland
St. John's School
Houston, Texas

Doris Glazer
Interboro High School
Prospect Park, Pennsylvania

Beth Goble
Lewisville Intermediate School
Battle Ground, Washington

Roz Goodman
Bering Strait School District
Unalakleet, Arkansas

Maryann Goree
Cascade Elementary
Chehalis, Washington

Sandra Gower
Cheney Junior High
Cheney, Washington

Mona Grandbois-Gallup
Westbrook High School
Sanford, Massachusetts

Velma Grant
Grandview High School Library
Hillsboro, Missouri

Marianne Gregersen
Bothell High School
Bothell, Washington

Mary Lou Gregory
Hoquiam High School
Hoquiam, Washington

Timothy N. Grey
Chehalis Middle School
Chehalis, Washington

Ruth Hadzor
Hillside Junior High
Boise, Idaho

Margaret Harrison
M. A. Jones Elementary #236
Jacksonville, Florida

Doug Hamilton
Evergreen School District
Vancouver, Washington

Doris Heaton
Hamilton County Unit #10
McLeansboro, Illinois

Susan H. Hendrickson
Centralia College
Centralia, Washington

Vera H. Henegar
Norwood Junior High School
Oliver Springs, Tennessee

Jan Herma
Forest Hills Elementary School
Broward County, Florida

Jacque Higdon
Millington Central Elementary School
Memphis, Tennessee

Jon M. Higley
Federal Way School District
Federal Way, Washington

Susan Hildes
Nassakeag Elementary School
Setauket, New York

Mary Jane Hill
Boise High School
Boise, Idaho

Carol Hole
Alachua County Library District
Gainesville, Florida

Janet Holt
H. Haller School
Sequim, Washington

Rainer Houser
Edmonds School District
Edmonds, Washington

Carol J. Hoyt
Hillcrest School
Bothell, Washington

Sharon Humphrey-Mason
Piscataquis Community High School
Guilford, Maine

Anne Hyland
Bexley City Schools
Bexley, Ohio

Lawrence Jaffe
Lionville Junior High School
Dowingtown, Pennsylvania

Barbara Johnstone
Office of the Superintendent of
    Public Instruction
Olympia, Washington

Camille Kiegel
Albuquerque Public Library
Albuquerque, New Mexico

Peggy Kimmet
Irving School
Bozeman, Montana

Jan King
Coweeman Junior High
Kelso, Washington

Richard C. Knudson
Snohomish High School
Snomish, Washington

Wilma I. Korb
Victoria, Virginia

Steve Kostanich
W. F. West High School
Chehalis, Washington

Carol Sue Kruise
Mary Hopkins Elementary
Littleton, Colorado

Richard Liles
Visalia, California

Debbie Locke
Westbrook High School
Westbrook, Maine

David Loertscher
Libraries Unlimited
Englewood, Colorado

Kathy Lowes
Gasconade R-2 Middle School
Cuba, Missouri

Roberta Margo
Virginia Public Schools
Virginia, Minnesota

Dori McCollum
Desert Hills Middle School
Kennewick, Washington

Linda L. McElwee
Pembroke Pines Elementary School
Pembroke Pines, Florida

Sue McGown
St. John's School
Houston, Texas

John McGrath
Oklahoma State Department of Education
Oklahoma City, Oklahoma

Glenda Merwine
Oak Harbor Junior High
Oak Harbor, Washington

Judith K. Meyers
Palatine School District
Palatine, Illinois

Duane Meyers
Metropolitan Library System
Oklahoma City, Oklahoma

Craig Miller
Lionville Junior High School
Dowingtown, Pennsylvania

Nancy Motomatsu
Office of the Superintendent of
    Public Instruction
Olympia, Washington

George Murdock
Walla Walla Public Schools
Walla Walla, Washington

Glenn Nelson
Columbus Public Library
Columbus, Nebraska

Karen K. Niemeyer
Carmel Clay Schools
Carmel, Indiana

Jean Novis
Spring-Ford Area School District
Collegeville, Pennsylvania

Dan Nusbaum
Hollywood, California

Catherine O'Hara
Middlebrook School
Wilton, Connecticut

Julianne Orlando
Sunset Elementary School
Tacoma, Washington

Mary Jane Palmer
Warren, Missouri

Ann Patterson
Lindsay Middle School
Hampton, Virginia

Sue Pattillo
Olympia High School
Olympia, Washington

Gloria Patton
Bennett and Olympic Elementary Schools
Chehalis, Washington

Donna Pettit
Fairwood Library
Renton, Washington

Vicki Phillips
Woodbrook Elementary—
    Clay City Schools
Carmel, Indiana

June Pinnell-Stephens
Fairbanks North Star Borough
    Public Library
Fairbanks, Alaska

Judy Radtke
Stanwood High School
Stanwood, Washington

Mary Lou Rakowicz
North Thurston School District
Lacey, Washington

Susan Rancer
McLeansville Middle School
Greensboro, North Carolina

Doris Robinson
Prospect Park, Pennsylvania

Ruth H. Robinson
James Solomon Russell Junior High
Lawrenceville, Virginia

Alvin G. Rogers
Rogers Middle School
Ft. Lauderdale, Florida

Ernestine B. Roller
Leesville Road Elementary School
Lynchburg, Virginia

Judy Rudolph
Grant Street Elementary
Port Townsend, Washington

Edith G. Sanders
Kirk Middle School
Euclid, Ohio

Luanne Scheuerman
West High School
Wichita, Kansas

Patricia L. Schmidgall
Fort Worth Public Library
Fort Worth, Texas

Peggy Agostino Sharp
Portland State University
Portland, Oregon

Dar Sisson
Grolier Books Representative
Seattle, Washington

Diane C. Skorupski
Liberty Elementary School
Tucson, Arizona

Mary Sleeman
Nordonia Hills Middle School
Northfield, Ohio

Steve Smith
Colton School District
Colton, Washington

Jeanette C. Smith
New Mexico State University Library
Las Cruces, New Mexico

Charlotte S. Spinks
Margate Middle School
Margate, Florida

Kathleen Spradlin
Hoquiam, Washington

Nancy Stanford
Bellwood Elementary School
Murfreesboro, Tennessee

Liz Stumpf
Clearfield Middle School
Clearfield, Pennsylvania

Roger B. Tanquist
Fairmont, Minnesota

Margaret Tassia
Millersville University of Pennsylvania
Millersville, Pennsylvania

Joie Taylor
Columbus Public Schools
Columbus, Nebraska

Laila M. Tedford
Marie Drake Middle School
Juneau, Arkansas

Margie Thomas
West Valley High School
Fairbanks, Alaska

Glenda L. Thompson
Green Hill School
Chehalis, Washington

Virginia S. Turner
Alexandria City Public Schools
Alexandria, Virginia

Sharon Tyler
Foster Elementary School
Sweet Home, Oregon

Edward O. Vail
Integrated Learning Systems, Inc.
Glendale, California

Diane Valvoich
The University School of Nova
Ft. Lauderdale, Florida

Ginny Vogel
Kamiakin Junior High
Kirkland, Washington

Volkert Volkersz
Machial Elementary School
Snohomish, Washington

David Wagar
Edmonds School District
Edmonds, Washington

Jim Weigel
Killingly Junior High School
Danielson, Connecticut

M. Jerry Weiss
Jersey City State College
Jersey City, New Jersey

Maureen White
Johnston Elementary
Abiline, Texas

Jean M. Wieman
Fullerton Union High School
Fullerton, California

Cheryl Wilson
Fegley Middle School
Portage, Indiana

Mildred M. Winslow
Retired Librarian
Kalamazoo, Michigan

Blanche Woolls
University of Pittsburgh
Pittsburgh, Pennsylvania

Sr. Georgia L. Yianakulis
Holy Rosary School
Seattle, Washington

Bobbie Zimmerman
Reed Junior High School
Loveland, Colorado

1 LIBRARIANS

In Antiquity

The Old Librarian's Almanack
Jared Bean, Philobiblos*
New Haven, Connecticut, 1773

Keep your Books behind stout Gratings, and in no wise let any Person come at them to take them from the Shelf except yourself.

Have in Mind the Counsel of Master Enoch (that most Worthy Librarian) who says: It were better that no Person enter the Library (save the Librarian Himself) and that the Books be kept in Safety, than that one book be lost, or others Misplaced. Guard well your Books—this is always your foremost Duty.

... So far as your Authority will permit of it, exercise great Discrimination as to which Persons shall be admitted to the use of the Library. For the Treasure House of Literature is no more to be thrown open to the ravages of the unreasoning Mob, than is a fair Garden to be laid unprotected at the Mercy of a Swarm of Beasts.

... No Person younger than 20 years (save if he be a Student, of more than 18 years, and vouched by his Tutor) is on any pretext to enter the Library. Be suspicious of Women. They are given to the Reading of frivolous Romances, and at all events, their presence in a Library adds little to (if it does not, indeed, detract from) that aspect of Gravity, Seriousness and Learning which is its greatest Glory. You will make no error in excluding them all together, even though by that Act it befall that you should prohibit from entering some one of those Excellent Females who are distinguished by their Wit and Learning. There is little Chance that You or I, Sir, will ever see such an One.

Let no Politician be in your Library, nor no man who Talks overmuch. It will be difficult for him to observe Silence, and he is objectionable otherwise, as well. No Astrologer, Necromancer, Charlatan, Quack, nor Humbug; not Vendor of Nostrums, nor Teacher of false Knowledge, no fanatick Preacher nor Refugee. Admit no one of loose or evil Life; prohibit the Gamester, the Gypsey, the Vagrant. Allow none who suffers from an infectious Disease; and none whose Apparel is so Gaudy or Eccentrick as to attract the Eye. Keep out the Light-witted, the Shallow, the Base and Obscene. See to it that none enter who are Senile, and none who are immature in their Minds, even tho' they have reach'd the requir'd Age.

---

*Edmund Lester Pearson, 1909

The Librarian's Life

The time *was* when a library was very like a museum and the librarian was a mouser in musty books. The time *is* when the library is a school and the librarian is in the highest sense a teacher, and a reader is a workman among his tools.
—Melvil Dewey

☆ ☆ ☆

In examining a candidate, having discovered that he is of good stock physically, and likely to bear the strain of continuous library service for a series of years; that he is accustomed to habits of order and punctuality; that he is studious and accurate, and above all amiable; the most thoro examination should be made of his intellectual ability.   —James L. Whitney, 1882

☆ ☆ ☆

Feel a real interest in the teachers and their work and never be too busy to pass a friendly word with them. Seek personal intercourse with the teachers, and explain the aim and value of the work you propose.
—H. P. James, 1896

☆ ☆ ☆

Dr. A. E. Winship, of Boston, followed with a vehement plea for teachers to own their own books. He said that much more could be done for teachers by librarians, than was being done. Librarians needed to get closer to the teachers and not go off by themselves, putting up barriers to keep the teachers out. Teachers were afraid of librarians, he was afraid of them himself. He believed no one could love and understand a good book who depended on the library for it.   —Notes from *The Proceedings of the State Association of Massachusetts*, 1897

☆ ☆ ☆

Ever since the librarian first realized that his mission was something higher than to be a mere custodian of books he has been earnestly and unremittingly seeking alliance with the teacher, his co-worker in the educational world.... He would doubtless claim, and could doubtless produce the strongest proofs of his claim, that the teacher has never yet met him half way.
—C. C. Young, 1899

☆ ☆ ☆

The demand is not so much for men and women of genius as it is for well-educated, thoroughly trained ones who know how to select books intelligently and administer them wisely.
—*Bulletin of the Iowa Library Commission*, 1901

The librarian should be estimated on the basis of ability to teach. Too frequently, the librarian's work is estimated as people estimate the work of a janitor. The low view holds the librarian responsible mainly for such things as keeping the books in their place and keeping off the dust.... He who creates and stimulates a desire for knowledge and places that knowledge within the reach of the seeker is doing the very best service as a teacher.
— J. N. Wilkinson, 1907

☆ ☆ ☆

Now let us consider deficiency in goodness and deficiency in beauty; or stated positively, badness and ugliness. These two things are confounded by many of us. Is this because the great majority of librarians to-day are of the sex that judges largely by intuition and often by instinctive notions of beauty and fitness? To most women, I believe all ugliness is sinful, and all sin is ugly.
— Arthur E. Bostwick, 1908

☆ ☆ ☆

When we went to the library we spoke to the librarian through a wire netting, and in our company manners asked for a book.
— Isabella Austin, 1909

☆ ☆ ☆

In a paper read by a school supervisor at a Pacific Northwest Library Conference: "You must make us feel our need for you. You must, if you please, intrude yourselves upon our notice. Generations of teachers have worshipped at the shrine of the textbook and can in no other way be reached. The ideals of education are broader, our needs are greater, and you have the materials to help us realize our needs." — *Library Journal*, September 1909

☆ ☆ ☆

A live, enthusiastic librarian is the best remedy ... a librarian shall rank with the high school teachers in educational preparation and personality, and be paid accordingly.
— Sophy H. Powell, 1917

☆ ☆ ☆

At first, we were delighted with the very evident popularity of the library. William Henrys and Mary Elizabeths flocked in precipitately at every vacant period.... Furthermore, we observed that our Mary Elizabeths and William Henrys loved to gather sociably around our tables, and that the limits of said sociability were largely in proportion to our ability to keep track of the room while keeping up our own rounds of desk and reference work.
— Lucile Fargo, 1920

☆ ☆ ☆

The school field has been largely dominated by women who are too self-sacrificing to demand due recognition.
— Mildred Frances Davis, 1923

I fear that we shall always have intolerance somewhere in education, and that, therefore, librarians ... should know as much as possible about all fields of knowledge and all books and how to lead the student from one book to another or from other books back to the one book, in order to find truth.
—Willis H. Kerr, 1925

☆ ☆ ☆

Librarians themselves should speak as seldom as possible and in as few words. Let me emphasize this. They should set the example to students in this respect.
—Mary T. Leiper, 1926

☆ ☆ ☆

The librarian is executive, counselor, critic, and supervisor.... But second only to the principal in the measure in which she may influence the success of the school is the patient woman who never runs out of smiles and has some interesting thing up her sleeve for every person in the building. Her success or failure will indicate the progress of the school.
—John Carr Duff, 1928

☆ ☆ ☆

The school of tomorrow will build its organization around the library and next to the principal the librarian will be the key person of the school.
—Helen Margaret Harris, 1929

☆ ☆ ☆

The children's librarian should be first of all well educated, refined—but not too limited in her tastes—possessed of sound common sense, clear judgment, and a keen sense of humor, gifted, it may be, with that kind of sympathetic second-sight that shall enable her to read what is often obscure in the mind of the child.
—Helen Martin, circa 1929

☆ ☆ ☆

I especially want the card catalog to prove useful so there I add helpful frills. On the author card for each book of fiction I type a brief sentence or so answering the question as to what the book is about.
—Azile M. Wofford, 1931

☆ ☆ ☆

And the old-type teacher, who throws up her hands in horror when she beholds the hum of industry in the classroom, finds her counterpart in certain librarians, who sadly shake their heads at the busy groups gathered round study tables in the up-to-date school library and long for the old days of pin-drop silence.
—Marjorie C. Dewire, 1931

☆ ☆ ☆

The librarian's relation to the teacher is analogous to that of the accompanist to the soloist.
—Hannah Bunge, 1933

The educational status of the school librarian with professional preparation was at first the cause of considerable bewilderment on the part of school superintendents and state educational officials.
— *Preparation for School Library Work*, 1933

☆ ☆ ☆

To me, the all important thing is to get the children in and give them all I can, all the library can. My desk is seldom straight. I do not check often enough on overdue books, fines, circulation. I have moments of great depression at my inefficiency. One can't do everything. One must do what seems best. — Phyllis R. Fenner, 1939

☆ ☆ ☆

Something for which I have lost all respect and which no longer seems very important — [is] circulation figures. I once held them in awe.
— Phyllis R. Fenner, 1939

☆ ☆ ☆

A teacher with full-time teaching duties who tries to look after the library on the side has been given an impossible assignment.
— *Schools and Public Libraries Working Together in School Library Service*, 1941

☆ ☆ ☆

First, the librarian no longer waits passively for teachers and students to call for service. In his new role, a major function of the librarian is to stimulate requests for service. *Second*, the library is expanding its range of materials, and this expansion may be expected to continue. *Third*, the librarian is assuming an increasingly important role in the school — as a teacher of students and as a coordinator and helper of teachers ... in the future schools may be expected to change their demands upon the library even more rapidly than in the past. — *Planning School Library Quarters: A Functional Approach*, 1950

☆ ☆ ☆

[Advice to children] Sometimes the librarian has a hard time keeping a balance between allowing the books to be used freely and keeping them in order and in good condition, which is a real necessity if the library is to go on being useful. If you understand that this is a real problem, and also remember that you are only one of many who ask not only questions, but also are likely to break rules by leaving things lying around, chattering to friends, misplacing books and forgetting to return them, you will realize that your librarian's efficiency and happiness are largely dependent on you.
— *Making the Most of School and Life*, 1952

☆ ☆ ☆

There can be few more unrewarding tasks for the educated man of curiosity than the routine duties of librarianship. — Angus Wilson

To be successful in a library you must make the librarians either respect or pity you.
— *18: The Teenage Catalog*

☆ ☆ ☆

The role of librarian has grown to encompass many additional responsibilities. We are now expected to be curriculum experts, library/information skills teachers, literature consultants, reference librarians, public relations officers, A.V. experts, office managers, computer teachers/technicians....
—Maureen White

Super Librarian

Contrary to popular opinion, not all librarians are barbarians.
—Randall McCutcheon

☆ ☆ ☆

Librarians—book lovers and people lovers.
—Richard Armour

☆ ☆ ☆

One bad school librarian can undo the work of a dozen good reading teachers.
—Jim Trelease

Booksellers are good at drinking; librarians are better.
— Eliot Fremont-Smith

☆ ☆ ☆

Librarians aren't all that smart, they just have their ignorance organized. — Found in a fortune cookie at Washington Library Association's "Legislative Day"

☆ ☆ ☆

It is just as far from the English classroom to the library as it is from the library to the English classroom. — Eleanor Ahlers

☆ ☆ ☆

A young male student at my school (Broadneck Senior High in Annapolis, Maryland), in a casual conversation about careers, the future, and so on, asked me if it didn't get a bit B-O-R-I-N-G being a librarian. I responded rather sarcastically, having long since tired of this implication, with: "Doesn't *any* job get B-O-R-I-N-G at times.... I mean how would you like to be a dentist, sticking your head in patients' mouths all day long???"

I could never have anticipated his reply. "Yeah, sure, but at least they make a lot of money!" — Renee Domogauer

☆ ☆ ☆

The county library supervisor was attending the University of Virginia a few years ago, working on her doctorate. Although this lovely lady had been a school librarian and a county library supervisor for some 15 years, when she walked into the UVA library to renew a book she completely drew a blank. She stood at the desk stammering, "I want to... to... you know, where you keep the book out for another two weeks...." — Deborah M. Cooke

☆ ☆ ☆

When a class from a neighboring elementary school made weekly visits to the branch public library in Minnesota where I worked, I became friendly with a 10-year-old girl who showed great interest in everything I said and did. One day my mother and sister stopped in for a short visit. When they left, the girl came up to me and asked me who those people were.

When I explained that they were my mother and sister, the girl looked at me in wide-eyed astonishment, and said, "*You* have a mother!"
— Jeanette C. Smith

☆ ☆ ☆

A slow-talking reference librarian took a telephone inquiry for a complicated recipe. The patron, we thought, was tediously writing down the ingredients and procedures as he read it. Halfway through, she exclaimed, "Not so fast, I haven't gotten the first part in the oven yet!"
— Mary Jane Palmer

I had worked in a junior high library for several years then moved to another building in the district. When I was back visiting and talking with the new librarian, a student came up to us and asked a question. In earlier times I would have directed the student to the third section of shelving by the wall. The new librarian, however, responded, "Meet me at the card catalog," and seized an opportunity for learning.

— Anne Hyland

☆ ☆ ☆

It didn't take me long in my first library position to discover that a quiet tomb was not inviting to my junior high clientele, and though no professors in my reference skills classes had hinted that I might benefit from the routine of the stand-up comic, I am finally admitting that a natural inclination to "play to the pits" helped me adapt a standard strategy to reference for the lunatic fringe known as "Junior High."

— Florence Anrud

☆ ☆ ☆

After I had taught in the elementary classroom for about 15 years, a friend talked me into applying for the job of school librarian when our librarian retired. I got the job and returned to school to get my librarian's certification. All went well for about seven years and then our library program was cut, and I was assigned the librarianship in two schools.

One afternoon a group of first graders arrived in the library of my new school to check out books. As I was stamping the book cards, one fell on the floor, and as I bent over to pick it up, I groaned, "O-o-oh, I must be getting old!"

A little first grader looked at me quite seriously and said, "Why, Mrs. Henegar, you can't be getting old! This is your first year here!"

— Vera H. Henegar

☆ ☆ ☆

One of our English classes was learning interviewing skills and I was asked to play the role of the interviewee. The assignment: Write an article describing something completely new you've learned about the person through the interview.

After describing my job, I talked about my very adventurous summers: I do long-distance biking, climb mountains, travel in Europe, and so on. In her paper, a young woman later wrote, "The interview provided a look into the life of a media specialist which I would have taken for dull and uneventful. Although most librarians are thought of as boring, Mrs. 'D' surprised me by showing that she is not like that. Her life is actually quite interesting."

— Renee Domogauer

☆ ☆ ☆

Imagine my surprise upon finding a slice of bacon in a book for a bookmark! Evidently the high school student hadn't eaten all his breakfast that morning.

— Mildred M. Winslow

One day the librarian noticed a conscientious volunteer struggling with a thick handful of book cards. She would pull out a card, look at it, and then find a place to reinsert it into the pack. An empty card sorter lay on the desk in front of her.

"Wouldn't it be easier to use the sorter?" the librarian suggested.

"I find," the volunteer answered deliberately, "that it's much easier to put the cards into the sorter if I get them in alphabetical order first."

—Dave Wagar

☆ ☆ ☆

The most shocked look I ever saw on a librarian's face happened one spring during the annual inventory. The inventory crew would mark the finished sections by placing slips of colored paper between the books. On the way into the librarian's office I found some extra colored strips and wadded them into a ball. As I sat down I tossed the ball into the wastebasket and informed her that I had helped her clean up by taking the slips that someone had mischievously placed throughout her shelves.

When she eventually realized that I had not ruined the inventory, she managed a big, relieved smile.   —Dar Sisson

The Trained Librarian

Instruction for Freshmen
University of Illinois
(Given to students in library classes, circa 1927)

1. Students are expected to have their problems ready to hand in on the day and hour designated by the instructor. A deduction is made from the grade for problems handed in late.

    Problems more than one week late, while accepted for credit, will not be eligible for a passing grade, except in the case of illness for which an excuse from the Dean of Men or the Dean of Women is presented, or by special arrangement made in advance with the instructor. Problems more than two weeks late, without the above excuse or arrangement, will not be accepted. No delayed problems will be accepted within the last week prior to examination, except in case of excused illness. Students delinquent in more than one-fourth of the weekly problems will not be given credit for the course.

2. All written work of the course, including weekly problems, quizzes and bibliographies, is to be done by each student independently. In asking assistance from the only authorized sources, viz., the instructors of the course and the reference librarians, the student must show his problem or state in advance that the question is from a library 12 problem.

    Students should be careful not to mark books with pen and pencil, since this gives the appearance of dishonorably helping one another and is also a violation of the Illinois statute forbidding the defacing of public property.

3. Answers to problems are to be written in the spaces provided between questions. Neatness, legibility, form, and completeness, as well as the correctness of the answers, are taken into consideration in the grading of the problems.

4. Students will find it to their own advantage to keep catalog drawers and reference books in order as they work with them.

The School Librarian
Library Manual for Virginia Public Schools

The good school librarian combines the best qualities of the teacher and librarian. She must have a sympathetic understanding of and the ability to make friends with children, as well as a wide knowledge of books and library techniques and a genuine desire to serve. To "sell" book service and a love of reading to children and teachers, the librarian must first sell the idea that she is glad to help patrons find a desired book, locate a bit of information, or even suggest a book to read "just for fun." Organizing the library efficiently is not enough. The effective school librarian will not only make her library the heart of the school, but she will win good will for libraries in general through her cooperation with other library agencies in the community and other civic organizations and through her contacts with patrons.

School librarians who have the requisite training are certified by the Virginia State Department of Education just as are other teachers. They are paid on the same salary scale as other teachers who have equivalent training and experience when they work for the same number of months per year. School librarians are not affected by the law regarding certification of public and college librarians passed by the 1936 General Assembly.

Regulations of the Virginia State Board of Education concerning the certification of teacher librarians are as follows:

Collegiate Professional certificate will be endorsed for teaching library science on presentation of six college session hours' credit as follows:

Cataloging and Classification..........................1 session hour

Reference and Bibliography............................2 session hours

Administration of School Library......................1 session hour

Adolescent Literature.................................1 session hour

Children's Literature.................................1 session hour

Total credits Library Science.........................6 session hours

—Virginia State Board of Education, August 1937

The education needed is the best attainable; a college training to begin with if possible; the wider reading and study in addition the better, for absolutely every item of information comes into play. It is specially important in most reference libraries to know German and French.... We greatly prefer college-bred women in selecting new librarians. — Melvil Dewey, 1886

☆ ☆ ☆

The time has passed when text-book instruction is satisfactory to either pupil or teacher ... the library [is] so great a necessity in the High School that in time a trained librarian will be deemed as essential in every High School as are trained teachers in the same school.

— *The High School Library: Suggestions for*
Organization and Administration, 1910

☆ ☆ ☆

First of all there is the preparation of the librarian. As long as the storehouse idea prevailed, there was no good reason why the librarian should be anything more than a clerk. But if the school library is to be an active educational agent, its presiding genius must be a specialist, and a thoroughly prepared one.   — Lucile F. Fargo, 1913

☆ ☆ ☆

In most library schools the technical requirements of library work seem to be overemphasized. The filing systems of a library can be readily mastered and are scarcely worth the attention they receive unless the librarian's profession is considered that of a clerk instead of an educational function.

— *The Children's Library: A Dynamic Factor*
in Education, 1917

☆ ☆ ☆

What school person of today isn't interested in credits? I have been amazed and chagrined to find that much of what I had thought two decades ago was about four years of college work is now rated as high-school requirement, and there are other changes. I'm all for the new order of things, but it is sometimes hard.   — Mary T. Leiper, 1926

☆ ☆ ☆

In 1925-26, the enrollment of fourteen accredited library schools totalled 553, of which 64 per cent were college graduates, 13 per cent had three college years and 11 per cent were without credit for a full year of formal education beyond high school. In 1930-31, the twenty-five accredited library schools enrolled 1,394 students, of which 4 per cent held master's or higher degrees, 68 per cent held bachelor's degrees, 20 per cent had three years of university college training, 7 per cent had less than three years at university or college, while only 1 per cent were high school graduates only.

— "Trends and Tendencies in Education for Librarianship,"
Library Journal, December 15, 1931

In a large library you will have to write down the number "M37j," the title of the book, and the author's name on a slip, and hand the slip to a page who will get the book for you. "M37j" is, you see, the number by which you *call* for the book.   —*School Library Year Book: Number One*, 1927

☆ ☆ ☆

Curricula for teacher-librarians are of two types: short curricula, and those not so short.   —*Preparation for School Library Work*, 1933

☆ ☆ ☆

The librarian should have a broad general education including literature, social science, physical sciences, and languages. Since the typewriter is used very much, skill should be acquired in high school. A knowledge of the fundamentals of bookkeeping will be helpful in figuring budgets and keeping records. Acquaintance with mechanical and architectural drawing will enable the librarian to read blue prints and to work intelligently with the architect in planning a building. These subjects also develop a sense of order, exactness, and neatness, which are useful attributes for the librarian. Art and home economics training can be employed in making the library attractive, and in arranging exhibits. Composition and journalism build a foundation for writing book notes and library publicity, and public speaking develops the librarian's personality and helps him in representing the library to the community thru formal speeches. Printing gives an understanding of the physical book. Debate develops ability in research.

—*The Student Library Assistant: A Workbook, Bibliography*
and Manual of Suggestions, 1934

☆ ☆ ☆

One of the major problems with the position of school librarian is the fact that the job has not been attractive enough to interest brilliant and creative people. Librarian training is comprised of a vast collection of minutia[e] administered by professors of education. The combination of trivia, taught in a setting of sterility, is more than creative minds can bear. The result is that most school library positions must be filled from the ranks of people whose training has been narrow, obstinate, and deeply steeped in irrelevant detail.

—B. Frank Brown. Reprinted by permission. Parker
Publishing Company, Inc., West Nyack, New York.
The Appropriate Placement School: A Sophisticated
Nongraded Curriculum. © 1965.

Librarians—As Seen by Others

What Teachers Think Librarians Do
(Teacher survey responses)

- Stamp out books.

- Type book cards and do other clerical jobs.

- File things.

- Guard the library's holdings.

- Purchase the materials for the library according to some secret formula known only to them and bringing about a balanced collection which contains nothing the teacher wants.

- Worry about overdue books.

- Worry about expensive materials circulating.

- Teach the use of the card catalog.

- Answer simple reference questions.

- Maintain strict discipline in the library.

- Have no responsibility for getting students through their high school education.

- Have a much easier day than teachers.

- Never have papers to grade or homework to prepare.

- Escape meeting the worst discipline cases in school because they are thrown out of the library if they misbehave.

- Pay little attention to school problems outside the library.

—R. R. Bowker, © 1975. Printed with permission.

Teachers feel that librarians are a pedantic, captious, fault-finding clique, who take special delight in pointing out how little teachers really know, and in exaggerating their eccentricities, and judging them as a class by a few erratic teaching freaks. —J. M. Greenwood, 1902

☆ ☆ ☆

I once asked a young woman who came for advice about taking up library work what had inclined her toward that particular occupation. She was quite frank with me; she said: "Why, my father and mother didn't think I was good for anything else." —Arthur E. Bostwick, 1915

☆ ☆ ☆

The work of the librarian is very hazily defined in the mind of the average layman. —Lucile F. Fargo, 1936

"What do you do up there all day?" is the question always asked of the school librarian. "I should think you'd be so lonesome, you'd plan to do some crochet or tatting or something!" This is a tale of what you actually will do as a school librarian, and you may supply the tatting in the place where you think it belongs!   —Irma M. Walker, 1919

Intellectually library workers are a highly selected group; they are on a par in intelligence with the student bodies of the very best universities and colleges, they excel the students in normal schools, and they make a very favorable showing as compared with those in other highly selected professions, such as law, medicine, and engineering.   —Fred Telford, 1925

☆ ☆ ☆

A librarian was complaining to a friend, "The trouble is, people don't understand my job. They think all I have to do is sit and check out books!"

Her friend replied, sympathetically, "Now isn't that silly? Of course you have to check them in, too!"   —Betty Jo Buckingham

☆ ☆ ☆

Our school has a shortage of parking spaces for faculty and staff. However, there are a couple of special people (the media specialist not included) who have reserved spots. Those are labeled Principal, Assistant Principal, Secretary, and Bookkeeper.   —Linda McElwee

Helping students find information is always enjoyable, but sometimes more enjoyable than others. Once a student, formerly from Iran, asked both librarians at different times for help in finding material on the same subject. After a lengthy search he told the second librarian, "See, the other one is smarter than you. She could tell right away there wasn't any information. It took you a long time." —Marianne Gregersen

☆ ☆ ☆

At a staff meeting held some years ago at a junior high school in southern California, the principal (a former physical education teacher) reported that he had discovered a serious problem with the new librarian. "I'm really concerned," he told us. "Every time I look in on her, she's reading!" —Edward O. Vail

☆ ☆ ☆

I work in a genealogy library. From time to time we receive such an inquiry as "Is this the gynecology library?," or when I tell someone that I work in a genealogy library the reply may be, "It must be satisfying to work with old people," confusing gerontology with genealogy!

—Camille Kiegel

☆ ☆ ☆

One trained librarian is quite enough for any library. Additional personnel should be clerks whose chief function is one of friendly assistance. These personnel must be willing to go to extremes in their efforts to assist students in their pursuit of knowledge.

—B. Frank Brown. Reprinted by permission. Parker
Publishing Company, Inc., Nyack, New York.
*The Appropriate Placement School: A Sophisticated
Nongraded Curriculum.* © 1965.

Librarian as Bookkeeper

Librarians always keep a supply of books on hand. It only follows that people confuse librarians with bookkeepers—or does it?

After a busy day in the elementary media center, I was greeted in the elementary parking lot by a third grader who had a very worried expression on his face. "Your car has been stolen!" he exclaimed.

Looking at my car parked just where I had left it that morning, I asked the boy where he got the idea that it was stolen. "Look!" he replied, pointing to the empty spot reserved for the school's bookkeeper.

Laughing, I pointed to my car.

"Don't media specialist and bookkeeper mean the same thing?" You keep all the books!" he quipped.

—Jan Herma

When I first came to Margate Middle School seven years ago as a new media specialist, I arrived with the enthusiasm and willingness to serve that one would expect. Along with the usual questions concerning the use of the library, I was very often asked by students to make change. I would comply whenever my wallet would allow, but soon questioned why so many students would come to me for this service. I soon learned that the students had been sent by their classroom teachers to the bookkeeper and the students naturally assumed that I was the keeper of the books, that is, the bookkeeper!

—Charlotte S. Spinks

When our school added vending machines in the lobby for after-school snacks, there was a sudden demand for change. A seventh-grade girl, wanting a soft drink, asked another student for change for a dollar. She was told to "go to the bookkeeper" for change, meaning the money handler in the office, but she came to me, the librarian. She asked for change, which I happened to have, so now she's convinced that I am a bookkeeper in every sense of the word.

—Jacque W. Higdon

Just What Is It That You Do, Anyway?

What does a librarian do all day? My nephew seemed to voice the opinion of the general populace when he asked, "Why do you need a master's degree just to sit behind the desk all day and tell the little kiddies where to find the Mother Goose book?"

How could he know that few "kiddies" were that specific! My requests in the elementary library were usually more like "Can I check out that red book Tracy had last time?"
— Velma Grant

I was recently asked how many years of schooling it takes "to get to sit behind the desk." How do you explain to a nonlibrarian what we do, what we study in library school, and why our job is supposedly important and more exciting than it seems? It is not easy to explain!
— Patricia L. Schmidgal

After the sixth graders are settled, the librarians resume their large group activities with second and fourth graders until interrupted by the telephone ringing. During browsing and check-out time, the two librarians are busy assisting the researchers who need help and also locating "mysteries" for the fourth graders whose teacher has made an assignment to read a mystery book, and failed to mention it to the librarians. Reading guidance and question answering are continued during this time period, in addition to the supervision of 70 + students using the library, as well as helping teachers who drop in for materials.

And this was just one 40-minute time period!
— Sue McGown

Reference

The Reference Librarian is Moses, come
to guide you out of the wilderness.
              —*18: The Teenage Catalog*

☆ ☆ ☆

Last week a girl asked for a book containing antidotes. I gave her one,
and she returned it saying she wanted the kind of antidotes you use for after-
dinner speeches.   —Mary T. Leiper, 1926

☆ ☆ ☆

Back in the days when Pat Lelatore and I were co-workers, and Timberline High School was still struggling with the "open concept," I was
challenged with one of the most unusual reference questions I've had in my
career:

Pat came to my desk and said, "Would you come talk to this student?
I've no idea where to find what he wants."

When I went out, the student said, "I want to know what this is."

He stood sideways, raised one leg, with knee bent, extended his arms,
bent at the elbows, with one wrist up, one down, threw back his head, and
opened his mouth.

I observed him a few seconds and said casually, "Oh, that's a heraldic
symbol. A Lion Rampant."

When I walked away there were some other mouths open, too.

              —Mary Lou Rakowicz

"Oh yes, a Lion Rampant!"

A student came into the library looking for a biography of Mr. Oni. The librarian tried to help, but they could find nothing in the catalog under Oni.

The librarian asked the student if he knew Mr. Oni's first name.

"Sure," he said, "It's Mark."   — Doris Dale

☆ ☆ ☆

Some years ago a ninth grader was searching the card catalog in our high school library. Asking him if I could help, I said, "What are you looking up?"

"Cleopatra," he replied.

"Why are you looking near the end of the alphabet? Cleopatra starts with *C*."

The reply: "I'm looking under her last name, Patra."   — Doris Glazer

☆ ☆ ☆

While participating in a Dewey decimal scavenger hunt, an eighth-grade boy, looking perplexed, stated that he had looked and looked for a book titled *Plays for Children*. When asked where he had been looking, he said, "In the 796s around football. It's about football plays, isn't it?"

— Judy Carlson

☆ ☆ ☆

A student asked me if I had a book about whores. I tried to decipher just what it was he needed to know about whores. He didn't seem very clear on the subject, so I asked why he needed information on the topic.

He told me that Mr. Porter, the eighth-grade English teacher, had sent him to the library.

I sent Mr. Porter a note, which came back stating that the boy was supposed to find information about Horace, the Roman poet!   — Anne Betts

☆ ☆ ☆

A student came into the Westbrook High School library one day and asked for a book about Eastern religion written by Sid Arthur. It took a few seconds for me to realize what book he wanted — *Siddhartha* by Hesse.

— Mona Grandbois-Gallup

☆ ☆ ☆

A first grader came into the library in December, and asked for the song "Good King Wenceslas." I began in the record collection, but could not find a Christmas record with that particular song on it.

I asked him if a copy of the sheet music would do. That was fine, he said, so I went to the 780s and began searching through the Christmas carol books. No luck.

When I asked further, he said that just a copy of the words would do, so I began searching encyclopedias and other source books.

Finally, he told me what he really wanted to know: "My teacher just wants to know how to spell 'Wenceslas.'"   — Candy Colborn

A student asked me if we had any material in the resource center on *flocculation*. I truthfully did not know the meaning of this word. I gave him such a startled look that he began to blush. Then I cautiously asked him if this was indeed a nasty word, and if he just wasn't telling me everything.

He turned a deeper shade of red and said that it wasn't a nasty word, and that, perhaps, I had some information on a "flocculating agent."

I seemed to get sillier as he repeated the word. It turned out to be a term in physics, and we did find material. But I spent the rest of the day asking any teacher that came into the resource center how their "flocculating agent" was. I was not the only one who didn't know what the term meant.

—Roberta Margo

☆ ☆ ☆

"This library doesn't answer all my needs," a student said. "I want books on déjà vu—you know, when a dream comes true."   —Marianne Gregersen

☆ ☆ ☆

Students often come into our junior high school library requesting a book they had checked out earlier in the year. Since they often don't recall the author or title, they frequently say, "Well, you know, it was a red [or blue, or green] book."

This used to drive me up a wall, but one day I realized I had sunk to that level when I heard myself asking a student, "Well, do you remember what *color* it was?   —Bobbie Zimmerman

☆ ☆ ☆

A student asked me, "Who won World War II?"

I was only joking when I answered, "The Japanese. That's why we drive so many of their cars." But he believed me.   —Dori McCollum

☆ ☆ ☆

Received at the Fairbanks North Star Borough Public Library:

NOTICE

please send me the book about where they talk about the guy that had a wax man grab him by the neck and the place where that one man leaped out of a jet and people found a par-ah-shoot and some mud covered money. also that part where they talk about sash-quoch, and the people involved it it. I cand remember the name of it. So if you can send it to me.

—June Pinnell-Stephens

A girl was having problems locating materials on her research topic and asked me for assistance. She told me she was trying to find information on why some elderly people experience memory lapses.

She informed me, "The library doesn't have anything on 'Old-Timers Disease.'"   —L. A. P.

☆ ☆ ☆

A fourth-grade teacher had assigned each child in her class a state to use as a topic of "research" in the school library. Each child was to find, among other things, the state flower, bird, and tree. After I had started the children on their project, a little girl came up to me and asked where she could find something about a "nõne tree."

Although I'd never heard of such a tree, I directed her to the section in the library where she could find books on trees. After a short time she returned, still unable to find this tree. I asked her to let me see the name of the tree, and she pointed in the encyclopedia where the summary of her state read: "tree—none."

Embarrassed, I realized I should "look before I leap."

—Mildred M. Winslow

☆ ☆ ☆

One of my first lessons in the importance of a reference interview occurred very early in my career. A student hurriedly appeared in the library one morning pleading for help to locate materials on gypsies. He could not stay, but promised to return after school and pick up anything we had as his report was due the following day.

In my eagerness to help I abandoned the policy to require greater effort on the student's part, and perhaps a penalty for someone who probably had waited until the last minute to visit the library.

Our collection was small then and it took me quite a long time to locate several passages in books and a periodical article on gypsies. I was indeed proud of my efforts and looked forward to the return of what would obviously be a most grateful student.

He did indeed appear at the end of the day and looked at our resources on gypsies. Instead of a grateful response, he told me the materials were useless as his report was on gypsy moths!   —Lawrence L. Jaffe

☆ ☆ ☆

A small girl came to the library and asked for "Genesis." I found a copy of the Bible, and asked her if that was what she wanted.

"No," she said. "It's the book that tells all about the tallest, and the heaviest, and the fastest."

—Candy Colborn

I was told early in my career that "librarians don't have to *know* everything—they just know *where to find it*."

This is theoretically true, but it does help to know some of the facts before we start looking. This was proven shortly after I opened our high school library when a thoughtful sophomore came in and asked, "Do you have anything on Euthanasia?"

Now if he had written his question down for me, the task would have been simplified considerably, because what I *heard* was "Youth in Asia"!

So, there followed a fruitless perusal of the card catalog for books on Asia, and then a scanning of their indexes for terms such as *Home Life, Children, Everyday Living, Social Life and Customs,* and so on. Not until I started through the *Y*s for the subject *Youth* did my patron clarify his request. (Sigh!) All in a day's work!

Thus, I have adopted as my slogan "Old librarians never die—they just CHECK OUT!"

— Velma Grant

Back in the days when *Sears List of Subject Headings* used *sects* instead of *cults* in their subject listing, a bashful young fellow ambled up to my desk and asked where he could find information about cults. He had not found anything under that subject heading. I told him to look under *sects*, but he thought I said *sex*, and blushed crimson. Realizing the problem, I spelled it out for him (while quietly cracking up). After that I always spelled *sects*, and furthermore, made sure the cross-reference card was replaced whenever it got swiped.　　　　　　　　　　　　　　　　　　　　　　　—Erma Berkley

☆ ☆ ☆

A group of students reported to our library media center one day to do follow-up research on a story they read in class. Danny, a seventh grader, approached me and said, "Mr. Weigel, I have to do some research on a dude."

Responding in the native lingo of the students, I asked, "Well, Danny, what dude do you have to look up?"

At this point, Danny handed me a slip of paper on which was written the name of his dude: Costa Rica!

Admirably restraining my urge to laugh, I said, "Danny, Costa Rica is not a dude. It's a country in Latin America."

At this point, Danny appeared totally bewildered. He paused a moment and finally said, in total amazement, "You're kidding!"　　　—Jim Weigel

☆ ☆ ☆

One has to use discretion as to how much help to offer college students in using a library. In this instance it was evident the young man wasn't finding what he wanted in the card catalog, so I asked if I could assist him.

He had seen *ibid.* so often in what he was reading, so he wanted to find what ibid had written. After explaining ibid. I suggested he not try to find *op. cit.* as an author, either.　　　　　　　　　　—Mildred M. Winslow

☆ ☆ ☆

A little boy came in and asked the librarian about dolphins. The librarian seized the opportunity to give him a minicourse in how to find things in the library using the card catalog, magazine index, pamphlet file, and on and on. Upon returning home that day his mother asked how his day had gone. "I learned more about dolphins than I ever wanted to know."　　　　　　　　　　　　　　　　　　　　　　　　—Ruth Hadzor

☆ ☆ ☆

A first grader requested an "elf" book one morning. I showed him a handy copy of *Brownies, Hush!*, but he wasn't interested. He gave me another chance, though, "You know, 'elf,' and Allen from outer space."

I didn't know, but persuaded him to check out *Alistair in Outer Space*. He left with the book and a puzzled look.

I spent the day wondering about an "allen elf" until a fellow teacher clarified: "He means ALF. Really, you librarians should watch more TV!"　　　　　　　　　　　　　　　　　　　　　　　　—Peggy Kimmet

While I was working with the second grade one day a boy asked me for the bear book with the medal on it. What he wanted was *The Biggest Bear* by Lynd Ward.   — Joie Taylor

☆ ☆ ☆

A note from a student:

Sea Urgent – I can't find that anywhere.
                                           — Marianne Gregersen

Research questions I've been asked:

- Was the tower of Hanoi anything like the Tower of Babel?
- Where did pizza come from?
- Can you find a picture of Gandhi's house?
- What was the name of the people the Spartans conquered and made slaves?
- I need a portrait of Homer.
- How much water supply does India have?
- Who was Henricopolis named after?
- What did Voltaire die from?
- What is the scientific name of the kind of hummingbird that only lives in Mexico?

                                           — Deborah M. Cooke

It is sometimes difficult to get users to ask for what they want. A fifth grader came in and said he wanted a biology book.

I hardly thought that was what he really wanted and asked him to tell me specifically what he was studying. Did he want a book about plants, or what?

He informed me he was not studying plants, so I asked if he wanted something on the human body.

He informed me that wasn't it, either. Then he said, "You know, a book about people." Then I knew that he meant *biography*.   — Carol Sue Kruise

☆ ☆ ☆

When I worked with the gifted/talented children a second-grade student came to me with a note. It read, "We are working on *Communities*. Please help J. C. find some information about communities in the library."

I asked J. C. what he thought might interest him. He wanted to research archaeology, particularly ancient Troy and Heinrich Schliemann.

I expressed doubt that archaeology would fit the community unit that the teacher had specified.

J. C. looked at me impatiently. "Well, archaeologists dig up old communities, don't they?"

J. C. did a terrific report on ancient Troy.   — Bobbie L. Brooke

A student asked, "Do you have the book *It Came Upon a Midnight Clear*? It's an old one."

After not finding the book I was informed, "It's by someone like Shakespeare. That's it! It's by Shakespeare."

It turned out that the student was looking for *A Midsummer Night's Dream*.   —Marianne Gregersen

☆ ☆ ☆

A boy walked up to me and asked, "Do you have old bones?" When asked to clarify his statement, he stated, "You know, *Old Bones the Wonder Horse*"!   —Mary Lou Gregory

☆ ☆ ☆

A student finally gave up in utter frustration trying to find Lincoln's Gettysburg Address and came to me for help. When I took her to the reference shelf and produced a copy of the speech, she started to laugh. "I thought the teacher wanted to know where Lincoln lived in Gettysburg!"

—Ruth Hadzor

Several years ago, a sixth-grade student came to the media center asking for information about Doctor Monroe. She didn't know anything about him (e.g., was he a Ph.D. or M.D.?) other than his name. We racked our brains trying to think who this doctor could be. No famous doctors came to mind.

Finally, through questioning, we discovered she wanted information about the Monroe Doctrine! Who says the reference interview isn't important?

— Cheryl Wilson

☆ ☆ ☆

When I was working in a junior/senior high school a student came in and asked for the "Harvard." Further questioning brought forth that the music teacher had sent him after the Harvard. I then knew he wanted the *Harvard Dictionary of Music*.

— Joie Taylor

☆ ☆ ☆

A note from a student:

I'm doing a report for biology. Where are all your books on homosexuals? I can't find much. Otherwise, I have to do my report on grunion. That's a fish! I think this would be more interesting.

— Marianne Gregersen

☆ ☆ ☆

Seen scribbled somewhere in the high school reference room:

ESCHEW OBFUSCATION

— John McGrath

☆ ☆ ☆

One day a sixth-grade boy asked for a book on "extra-terresticles." I asked him to repeat his request. Again he asked for a book on "extra-terresticles." He insisted that a friend had checked out such a book from my library, and now he wanted it.

I asked if he meant extraterrestrials.

He said, "Yeah ... extra-terresticles ... where is it?"

— Kathy Lowes

☆ ☆ ☆

The freshman English teacher at our high school requires book reports every nine weeks. One of his requirements is that the book be at least 200 pages in length. One day a freshman student came in and asked me to help him find a long book. In fact, he wanted the longest book we had. I told him it would probably be *Gone with the Wind*, or one of James Michener's books. I also told him that I was surprised and yet pleased at his request. (I usually am looking for books exactly 201 pages and no longer!)

He then informed me that he needed it for biology—he was going to use it to press his leaves.

— Cathy Baker

☆ ☆ ☆

A grade-school boy came up to the children's librarian's desk and seriously asked, "Where do you keep the *good* books?"

— Donna Pettit

A student from a science class came to the library and told me that his teacher assigned him a brief report on a scientist. After a short conversation it became obvious that he did not know the name of any scientist. I suggested that he might consider doing his report on Einstein, and off he trudged to the encyclopedias.

Later he approached me with the *S* volume of an encyclopedia. "Are you looking under *scientist*? I asked.

"No," he replied. "I'm looking under *Stein*."   — Irene Clise

☆ ☆ ☆

I have been asked, "Where are your books on

- building your body *fast*?"
- Monday Night Football?"
- barbed wire?"
- pierced ears?"
- how much music affects your sleep?"
- first aid for snakes?"

   —Marianne Gregersen

Overdues

A patron expressed her surprise that we had not received her overdue book. Puzzled, she exclaimed, "I don't understand.... I put it right in the book suppository outside"!   — Paula J. D'Ambrosio

☆ ☆ ☆

One young man returned his book which was about five months overdue. When I asked him why he waited, he replied, "My cat died, my canary got sick, and my dog ran away from home."

"I'm sorry to hear that, but why did you just now return the book?" I asked.

His reply: "My cat died, my canary got sick, and my dog ran away...."

Oh, well ... what could I say?   — Edith G. Sanders

☆ ☆ ☆

After several weeks of denying responsibility for a book he had checked out, a sixth-grade boy stomped into the library, slammed the book into the book return, and proclaimed, "See, I *told* you I didn't have it!"

   —Candy Colborn

☆ ☆ ☆

Response about an overdue book from a third grader: "Well, I left my book in the car—and Dad sold the car."   —Anne Hyland

As I was resting on my laurels thinking I had heard every excuse from A (it is at my aunt's abode) to Z (it's stuck in my jacket zipper) for not returning a library book, imagine my surprise when a student came in one day and apologetically said he could not return his overdue library book because it was "in jail."

It seems his brother was in possession of the aforementioned book when he was arrested by the local constable. A telephone call confirmed that the book lay in the property room of the local jail.

Incidentally, the title of the book is *Creative Projects Using Power Tools.*
                                                                    — Judy Carlson

These are a few favorite excuses for overdues out of the millions we hear. "I don't have an overdue book. I remember that I brought it back two weeks ago and put it in the box. The girl behind me took it and checked it out." Also, "I left my magazine on the bus and my bus driver turned it in at the high school." Even after you call the high school and verify that it has not shown up, the student keeps telling you the same story.

My school is housed in two buildings that are located about a mile apart. Therefore, I have two separate media centers. "My brother turned it in at the other building" is one of our most frequently heard excuses.
                                                                    —Margaret Harrison

☆ ☆ ☆

A first-grade girl quite seriously explained to my library aide that she hadn't brought back her library book that day because her daddy had come home drunk the night before and peed on it, and her mother was trying to wash it. The book, by the way, showed up the next week seemingly none the worse for wear.
                                                                    — Judy Rudolph

A letter from a former student who failed to return her library books, and a school librarian's reply:

Fullerton Union High School Library
201 E. Chapman Ave.
Fullerton, CA 92634

Subject: Gross Negligence

Gentlemen:

As a student of Fullerton Union High School, graduate class of 1973, I quite apparently "took" my studies seriously.

During a recent move I noted that the enclosed book was not properly in my possession for two reasons: (1) the enclosed was "not to be taken from this room," and (2) I am certain it is seriously overdue.

I am sure that I earned commendable marks on the report submitted for which this book was used, since my academic scores were always satisfactory. However, in the ethics department, I am afraid I have miserably failed.

Please accept this returned book as an effort of mine to correct this gross error, and the enclosed check as an effort to compensate you for the time and effort expended, once upon a time, looking for this book.

Our best to *every* graduate class of FUHS.

Sincerely,

Pamela L. Christian

Dear Mrs. Christian:

It is always gratifying to see that our former students not only took their studies seriously but are now "giving back" to their alma mater and the FUHS community.

You may be interested in knowing that the previous librarian alerted me to this particularly serious situation prior to my accepting this position. I decided to take the job anyway, having full faith that any FUHS grad would resolve the sad state of affairs at some point during my tenure.

Rather than apply your generous gift to the considerable fine which has accrued, we have decided to select an appropriate title for addition to our library collection — perhaps a copy of *Kidnapped*.

Also as a result of your extensive efforts, we can now go ahead and schedule our June "Celebration for Returnees" which had been postponed repeatedly since the spring of 1973. You are cordially invited to attend to receive our thanks in person.

Sincerely,

Jean Wieman, Librarian
Fullerton Union High School

Library Lessons and Storytelling

The tendency of textbook teaching of the schools is toward deadening the young mind to that feeling for literature, and alienating it from books by prejudice born of wrong impressions at the beginning. —F. N. Larned, 1897

☆ ☆ ☆

There has been too much of the giving of formal "reference courses" and not enough practical instruction on the part of teachers in connection with regular work.... How many times have you had to remind your seniors that Andrew Jackson cannot be found in *Who's Who*, in spite of the fact that in their sophomore reference they learned (or at least you told them) that this volume was for contemporaries only. —Lucile F. Fargo, 1923

☆ ☆ ☆

During a lesson on locating easy fiction books by their spine labels I couldn't help laughing when first graders discovered the *T* section and immediately exclaimed, "Wow! Look at all the books about E.T.!" I decided that *easy* books should have spine labels with only the first letter of the author's last name and no *E* above that letter. —Roz Goodman

"Look, E.T.!"

Teaching library skills in isolation is like having a kid waving his arms and legs while sprawled over a table, then saying, "Remember to do this when you get into a pool."

— Betty Buckingham

☆ ☆ ☆

I was doing a lesson for the sixth and seventh grades on how to look at a fiction book and decide whether to read it or not. They had to look at the characters, the setting, and the plot, and then make a judgment based on a scale of 1 to 10. If they circled 10, that would be the highest or most interesting book, and 1 would be a total rejection—they absolutely would not read it.

A couple of weeks later a seventh grader came into the library and said, "Mrs. Rancer, if I were to rate this book on the *Richter* scale, I'd give it a 10! It was a very interesting book."

It must have also been a very "moving" book!

— Susan P. Rancer

☆ ☆ ☆

Third graders in an Oregon coast school were instructed about the card catalog and its many uses. The librarian was well pleased with the lesson and with the progress the students had made. Two youngsters approached the librarian with the *X* drawer in hand, which happened to be without its cards because of an overhaul in progress, and said with absolute innocence, "How come we don't have one 'X-rated' book in the library?"

— Dar Sisson

"Look!! X-rated books!"

A seventh grader's definition on a library skills quiz:

interlibrary loan: "You lend the prity libraryan to somebody."

— Debbie Locke

A number of years ago when I was a librarian in an elementary school I used creative dramatics with the lower elementary classes to act out various stories and books. One of the students' favorites was *Where the Wild Things Are*. I always tried to give parts for every child, and stressed that when they were a character, they were no longer little boys or girls. Even if they were the trees in which the wild things played, they were very special trees which could hear only me. It was stressed that everybody should try their hardest to assume his or her character, and could only return to their original forms after I said the magic words.

During the story one darling little girl, who happened to be a tree, vomited, then immediately stood up again as a tree. Before I could reach her she vomited a second time, and once more returned to a tree. I was at her side when she vomited for the third time, and watched her return to character once more as a very messy tree.

Everyone in the class remained in character, but looked at me pleadingly. I did not miss my cue. I said the magic words, and Max, the wild things, and the forest were little girls and boys again, very somber little boys and girls, and returned to their room with their books. —L. A. P.

☆ ☆ ☆

To reinforce the idea that biographies are generally about famous people, I asked a fourth-grade class, "Would there be a biography about *me* on our shelves?"

"No," came the answer, and I called on one girl to explain why not.

How surprised and flattered I was when she answered, "You're too young!" — Judith Alexander

☆ ☆ ☆

I had assigned my 99-percent-Anglo fifth graders a Black History Month project. They were to take one biography of a famous black American from the *World Book*, and create either an original paragraph or skit using that information. One student chose Charlie Parker. One of his final sentences came out, "Charlie Parker, a thelonius monk, helped found the bebop movement in jazz." — Candy Colborn

☆ ☆ ☆

"You can't be finished reading, I haven't started listening yet," was in response of my reading to the students. — Ann Patterson

☆ ☆ ☆

I was reading *Fat Cat* to a kindergarten class. In the story, the cat eats everyone with whom he comes in contact, and he grows fatter and fatter. Finally, the fat cat meets a parson with a crooked stick. Knowing that "parson" was an old-fashioned term, I asked the class if they knew what a parson was. Several guesses were made, and then Brandi raised her hand and said, "I *think* it is something like a human being." — Ernestine B. Roller

One day I did some storytelling for one of the first-grade classes in Columbus. "I didn't like that story. I loved it!!! I can't believe you read that story without looking."

— Glee Nelson

A letter from one of my third-grade students at the end of the year:

Dear Mrs. Book,

I love the library. I like it when you read to us. I especially like it when you use all your voices. But I really like your shoes.

Love,

Jason

(They always sat at my feet for stories.)

— Bobbie L. Brooke

"Love those shoes."

As an elementary school librarian, I try to read stories to my students in an entertaining manner. Voice changes, props, outlandish facial expressions, mannerisms, and accents are nothing new to my young scholars.

I was reading *The Story of Ferdinand*, by Munro Leafe, in grand style to a class. My Spanish accent was impeccable, down to my perfectly rolled *r*'s.

After I finished, Donald raised his hand and said, "I've heard that story. My teacher read it to us last year."

Raising my head in a proud, regal gesture, I said, "Oh, really? And did *she* use a Spanish accent when she read it?"

Donald looked at me and said, very seriously, "No. She read it so we could understand it."

— Wilma I. Korb

☆ ☆ ☆

It was a typical Christmas week in my first grade class. I read at "shared book experience" time the poem, "'Twas the Night before Christmas."

For the next three days Russell continually asked me to read the story about the man who vomited the ribbon. I finally asked him to bring me the book because I wasn't sure what he was talking about.

Russell brought me "'Twas the Night before Christmas," and I started to read it again to the class. When I read, "I went to the window and threw up the sash," Russell said, "There! There! That's the man who vomited the ribbon!"

— Cheryl Budgett

While teaching a fifth-grade class how to use indexes I used the subject Crabs on the worksheet. While listing other possible subjects, such as Hermit, which we could search to find more about crabs, one boy raised his hand and offered, "Mr. Sage says you get crabs from toilets."

—Marianne Candioglos

☆ ☆ ☆

Who is Warren E. Burger?

Three years ago, I ran a trivia contest at Piscataquis Community High School in observance of National School Library Media Month. One of the questions, "Who is Warren E. Burger?" brought the following response from a freshman student: "The founder of Burger King."

I've often wondered if the former Chief Justice would be as amused as I was to learn of his notable achievement!   —Sharon Humphrey-Mason

☆ ☆ ☆

All elementary librarians know that there is a direct correlation between the book you read to a class and the circulation of said book. I was doing a unit on Tomie de Paola with second graders. The story for the day was the *Clown of God*, the poignant tale of the little juggler who found that after many years of delighting crowds with his act he could no longer perform as he wished. After living as a recluse for many years, he entered a church to find a tearful statue of the Holy Mother and the Christ Child. His final act was to entertain the child and bring a smile to his face.

The next morning, a small boy came running into the library crying, "Mrs. Carlson, can I check out that book you read yesterday ... you know, *Juggling for Jesus?*"!

—Bev Carlson

During story time in our media center the students sit in the story well, where there is an emergency fire exit. One very cold day I said to a class, "Today we will not sit in the story well because there is a big draft coming in the door."

After the story and book selection, I started to line up the students and one boy protested, "But the giraffe hasn't come yet." I had him repeat this several times because I insisted I had not said this.

Finally another student spoke up, "You said we couldn't sit in the story well today because a big giraffe was coming through the door!"

— Jane Cribbs

☆ ☆ ☆

Several years ago (during the summer), I was school librarian for one of the elementary schools in my district. During story hour I told the story of *Sylvester and the Magic Pebble*. After telling the story I asked the fourth-grade class to share one wish with their classmates: "If you had only one wish in the whole wide world from this magic pebble, and knew that this wish could come true, what would be your wish?"

We went around the room and some said they would want money, or a nice big house for mom, or would buy this or that.

However, one little boy said, "If I had one wish, I would wish for the Dallas Cowboy cheerleaders."

After he made his statement I quickly moved to the next student. Someone later told me that I should have asked the boy what he would have done with the cheerleaders.

— Edith G. Sanders

☆ ☆ ☆

Sean was one of our favorite students, even if he could never return anything on time. Then one day while I was contemplating how to discard boxes of old record albums I had an idea that would get rid of the records, teach Sean a lesson, and have fun, all at the same time.

I snooped around and located Sean's locker. While he was in class I filled his locker to the brim with old records. I placed a note in his locker telling Sean, "Since you like our materials so much that you never want to part with them, you may keep these records forever." I was so pleased with myself.

My first hint that something was amiss was when I looked out the library's windows and saw records sailing through the halls like Frisbees. My extremely upset assistant principal soon ran into the library and wanted to know if we knew the name of the idiot who had taken records from the library and had stuffed them into a student's locker.

Oops!

— L. A. P.

In telling stories to children, I don't think it is necessary to explain every big or unfamiliar word unless it has a direct bearing on the story. One story I was using with a second-grade group had the word *famine* which was necessary for the children to understand if they were to get the idea of the story. Therefore, I asked if anyone could tell me what a famine was. A little girl raised her hand and said, "It's when a father and mother and children live together in a house." So much for famines!   —Mildred M. Winslow

☆ ☆ ☆

I always think that I do a good job of discussing the Caldecott Award medal with my first-grade classes, but a second-grade teacher told me that prior to reading a recent Honor book to her class she held it up and asked if anyone knew what the medal meant. A boy blurted out, "It means it's been through the wars!" (I wonder if that's how the Caldecott committee feels by the time they've reached a decision.)   —Judy Rudolph

PART 2   FREE PEOPLE— FREE LIBRARIES

The Library

My own personal experience may have led me to value a free library beyond all other forms of beneficence. When I was a boy in Pittsburgh, Colonel Anderson of Allegheny—a name I can never speak without feelings of devotional gratitude—opened his little library to boys.... I resolved that if ever wealth came to me it should be used to establish free libraries, that other boys might receive opportunities similar to those for which we were indebted to that noble man.   — Andrew Carnegie

☆ ☆ ☆

Never lend books, for no one ever returns them: the only books I have in my library are books that other folk have lent me.   — Anatole France

☆ ☆ ☆

Now ... we are still more or less under the influence of the old traditional view of the library as a storehouse of books.   —H. E. Scudder, 1893

☆ ☆ ☆

A teacher who goes to a library and finds its privileges much hedged about with rules and regulations will perhaps use it occasionally, certainly not often.   —*Public Libraries*, June 1896

☆ ☆ ☆

A library should be to the boy a place of pleasure, first, and a place of education, second.   —L. E. Stearns, 1897

☆ ☆ ☆

The school library is no longer a luxury, but is rapidly becoming an essential element in the equipment of every school.
—*Public Libraries*, September 1897

The free use of libraries undirected is a pernicious practice. It is far better to have the teachers select and restrict the reading of the pupils. Many a complaint of poor work is due to the fact that the mental energy of the pupil is appropriated to reading books of no value in his educational progress, leaving him dull and listless for the specific work of the schools.

—Doctor Brumgaugh, 1900

☆ ☆ ☆

The dangers of the new library work are those of distraction. Pupils who consult shelves for one topic are often led by a more superficial interest to gratify lower tastes. —G. Stanley Hall, 1905

☆ ☆ ☆

It is usually the best policy to purchase books through the local book store, provided the book store can furnish the books practically as cheap as book stores in large cities. —*A Library Primer for High Schools*, 1917

☆ ☆ ☆

Books should not be classified by title. Examine the table of contents, read the preface or introduction, and if necessary, read parts of the book, especially the conclusion. The table of contents will not always give the character of the book. Usually, the preface contains a statement of the author's purpose in writing the book and his theme.

There are two systems of classification in use: the Expansive and the Decimal.... —*A Library Primer for High Schools*, 1917

☆ ☆ ☆

Another of my boys, so his father tells me, thinks that the library economy would be greatly improved, if the publisher would stamp the classification number on the back of the book and on the title page when it is published! This opened endless possibilities. The publishers might send the skeletons of their books to a committee of the American Library Association, who would classify them as is done in the book list—and how it would simplify everything if catalog cards could accompany each book! That is too much to dream—but the fact of the boy thinking of it was interesting.

—Marion Lovis, 1920

☆ ☆ ☆

The school system that does not make liberal provision for training in the use of libraries fails to do its full duty in the way of revealing to all future citizens the opportunity to know and to use the resources of the public library as a means of education.

—*National Educational Association Guidelines*, 1921

☆ ☆ ☆

There are really only two objectives the library has: to get children to come to the library and to keep them coming. —Phyllis R. Fenner, 1939

If we are to have an educated and informed population, we need a strong and open library system, supported by a committed administration. We cannot call for a revival of quality education in America and close our libraries. We cannot ask our children to learn to read and take away their books.   — Jimmy Carter

☆ ☆ ☆

When our genes could not store all the information necessary for survival, we slowly invented brains. But then the time came, perhaps ten thousand years ago, when we needed to know more than could be conveniently contained in brains. So we learned to stockpile enormous quantities of information outside our bodies. We are the only species on the planet, so far as we know, to have invented a communal memory stored neither in our genes nor our brains. The warehouse of that memory is called a library.

— Carl Sagan

☆ ☆ ☆

A library is thought in cold storage.
— Herbert Samuel (also attributed
to Samuel Johnson)

☆ ☆ ☆

If truth is beauty, how come no one has their hair done in the library?   — Lily Tomlin

☆ ☆ ☆

Libraries are too seldom used, and are even more seldom used effectively.
— M. Chandler Elliott

☆ ☆ ☆

If public schools are for formally directed education, then libraries are for self-direction.   — Stephen Robinson

☆ ☆ ☆

The library media program is at least as important as a varsity sport. — Rainer Houser

☆ ☆ ☆

The library is the most important center of the universe to tap.   — M. Jerry Weiss

☆ ☆ ☆

Make the library ... not just a place to send bright kids or trouble-makers, or the location of once-a-year lectures on the use of the card catalogue and the mysteries of the Dewey Decimal System.
— *The English Teacher's Handbook*

The library is not a serious place. [In fact,] the library is a maelstrom. When I talk to students, I tell them, plunge into it like a bunch of apes; like you were climbing Kilimanjaro or going to Alpha Centauri. Libraries are joyful, explosive, hysterical! They're playgrounds!   — Ray Bradbury

☆ ☆ ☆

It was my first job after receiving my library-media certification. I knew the library had been cataloged by nonlibrarians, but I was not quite prepared for the creative cataloging I encountered. I *knew* that Ann Nolan Clark's classic *In My Mother's House* was in this library somewhere, but the author card was not in the catalog, and the title card eluded me. One day, weeks later, I encountered it in the *H* drawer, the title neatly typed in red ink: "House, mother's, in my."   — Candy Colborn

☆ ☆ ☆

Once while checking catalog cards, back in the days when catalog cards were typed instead of being picked off the computer, I found a few interesting typos:

"A Shitory of ..." instead of "A History of ..."

"Boobs-Merrill Pub. Co." instead of "Bobbs-Merrill"

— Erma Berkley

☆ ☆ ☆

There are exceptions to every rule. The catalog is in alphabetical order — except for History, which uses country and time. Sears must have been a history major.   — Anne Hyland

☆ ☆ ☆

At my first high school library job, which was in Nebraska, I went to the card catalog and discovered 250 cards filed under *The*.

At my second high school library position in Colorado I went to the card catalog and found three copies of *A Tale of Two Cities*, by Charles Dickens. There was one copy in the 840s, one in the 944s, and one in fiction: The same book in three different locations!   — Don Dresp

Primary Classification

Symbols used to place primary books into subject areas:

a. C   Cowboys.

b. CH   Community helpers.

>   E   Easy readers. (snuck in because of decadent influences from the outside)

c. H   Holidays and special occasions.

d. HS   Home and school.

e. I   Indians.

f. M   Miscellaneous. Readers and books that include several subjects.

g. PA   Pets and animals.

h. PB   Picture books.

i. SS   Science and seasons.

j. T   Transportation.

The list is from *Library Services and Procedures Handbook*, Edmonds School District, 1958. Undoing these classifications for 22 libraries took four years.　　　　　— Dave Wagar

Does our organization of materials reflect the social environment? Whose? Is the native American still in 970.1 on a reservation, or with the history of states — both far away from 973, and the rest of America's history? Is there still a 301.451 ghetto on the shelves — a peculiar thing of social inquiry where minorities are confined — all the way across the room from the "regular history" of people?　　　　　— Anne Hyland

☆ ☆ ☆

The following catalog cards came from a small school library in "bush" Alaska. The library had a very peculiar organizational scheme — the aide didn't realize that the Dewey numbers meant anything, so she assigned three numbers at random to the nonfiction.　　　　　— June Pinnell-Stephens

F
HICK   NORMAN G HICKMAN

THE QUINTESTALIAL QUIZ BOOK

F
HEM   ERNEST HEMINGWAY

A FAIR WELL TO ARMS

It was my first week in the 20-year-old school library. I knew I had seen Robert Lawson's *Ben and Me*, but I looked in vain through the *L* section of fiction, and could not find a check-out card to explain its absence.

I later discovered it had been rebound, and the dark red binding bore the call number *Fiction—A*.

I couldn't imagine why. It is the story of the life and times of Ben Franklin, written by his friend, the mouse, Amos. The workers at the bindery simply read the title page, as any good cataloger would do.

—Candy Colborn

☆ ☆ ☆

When I start to think that it all is so easy, and students don't think, I often remember this question, "Why can't I find Verbs in the card catalog?"

—Anne Hyland

☆ ☆ ☆

A billing to Port Angeles High School Library, Port Angeles, Washington:

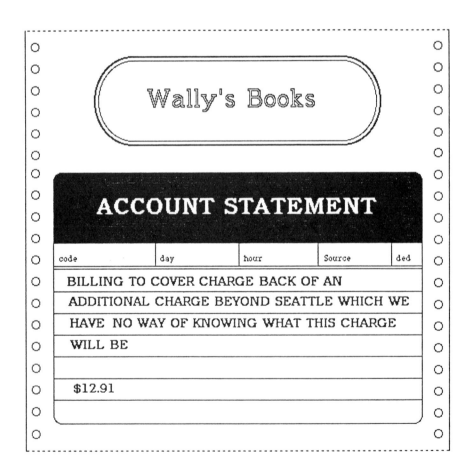

code	day	hour	Source	ded
BILLING TO COVER CHARGE BACK OF AN				
ADDITIONAL CHARGE BEYOND SEATTLE WHICH WE				
HAVE NO WAY OF KNOWING WHAT THIS CHARGE				
WILL BE				
$12.91				

—Erma Berkley

I was so excited to be able to order 15 more drawers for the card catalog. The size of the book collection had almost doubled from 6,000 books to 10,000 books over a period of 18 months. There were plenty available shelves to hold the new books, but the 30-drawer catalog was packed to the limit. The students could not even read the cards because the drawers were so full. When the order for the drawers was placed, I felt as if a great burden had been lifted from my shoulders.

But my ecstasy did not last long. When the drawers arrived, they were walnut stained instead of light oak stained. I telephoned the company about the problem and they promised to remedy the situation. Days—weeks—a month passed. I telephoned the company again. They were confused because according to their records shipment had been made. The company promised to check into the problem.

In a couple of days I received a phone call from the shipping company responsible for sending the merchandise. It seemed that the shipping company had confused my last name (Driver) with the city where the drawers were to be delivered. The card catalog drawers were sitting in a warehouse in Driver, Arkansas, unable to be delivered to the correct school. Within the week the new, light-oak-stained catalog drawers finally arrived.

—Mary Driver

☆ ☆ ☆

We have warning signs by our security system which mention caution to people wearing pacemakers, and also that the system can damage or erase videotapes, discs, and cassettes.

A pregnant student and her boyfriend were heading for the exit when the boy spotted the sign. He stopped the girl, and then asked me what the system would do to the unborn baby.

I assured him the baby would not be hurt, but he was doubtful and insisted I let them out the back door.

As I later thought about this incident, it occurred to me that a more common reaction to the suspicion that a magnetic field could erase babies might be for boys to march their girlfriends back and forth through the exit.

—Linda Brake

☆ ☆ ☆

Against my wishes, construction plans called for a reading pit to be placed in our middle school library. I was concerned about monitoring middle school students who, as we all know, can frequently become squirrelly under the most supervised occasions, but another problem became even more troublesome. Leaks and floods continually filled the reading pit with water.

Once when returning to school after a vacation, the library was inundated with countless little green frogs which either hatched from, or gravitated to, our reading pit!

Even though the frog problem has long since been rectified, our library has adopted the frog as its mascot.

—Dori McCollum

Olympia High School's library was constructed a number of years ago on the second floor above regular classrooms. The only access to the library is the stairs. Enterprising country youths, knowing that cows only walk up stairs, not down them, decided to place a cow in the library for the weekend. The project was successful and the mess was astronomical.　　—Sue Pattillo

☆　☆　☆

Book titles *do* become awkward at times when used in sentences! I find this especially true on "overdue" notices. For instance, how do you tell a high school girl that her *Teenage Pregnancy* is overdue? Or that *Death and Dying* was due yesterday?

The topics high school students choose for their term papers can also get personal. When I have 25 kids in the library doing research on various topics, I find additional material that someone asked me for earlier and may not remember which one asked for it, so I punctuate the hour with inquiries such as:

- "Who's doing 'abortions'?"
- "Who's on 'drugs'?"
- "Who's working on 'divorce'?"
- "Who's in 'cults'?"
- "Who's in 'secret service'?"
- "Who has 'child abuse'?"

I always get an answer, and perhaps a laugh or two, but it relieves the tension, and students know there's help available.　　—Velma Grant

☆　☆　☆

During my own checkered past, while I was still in high school, several members of my class used to find great glee in going into the library and changing the signs on the book racks that told which Dewey numbers each shelf held. I always remember one of the girls getting caught because she was only four feet tall and the principal discovered that most of the numbers that were fairly low on the racks had been changed. Actually, that pretty well ended the changing of the numbers for the rest of the year.

　　—George Murdock

☆　☆　☆

The faculty was asked to write up a description of their area of work. The following was not the description submitted, but one that felt good to write.

The Instructional Media Center (IMC) is an educational babysitting instrument. It is an integral support component of the total teaching-learning enterprise which includes: garbage pickup, locker checks, custodian answering service, desk cleaning service, errand service, and an all-around handyperson. Therefore, the function of the IMC program is to support (upset) teachers, to implement (bathroom privileges), to enrich (students with chemistry problems), to vitalize (Monday blues), and to humanize (just take a look at middle school students' dress code) the educational program as we strive to attain excellence in content (we need more romance novels), process, and product.

　　—Elizabeth Beckman

Budgets and Costs

A Library Primer for High Schools
1917

A.L.A. Booklist — $1.00 per year. This is the best source from which to select current books. The purpose of this periodical is to help small libraries make selections for purchase. Brief descriptions and evaluations are given.

Magazines

A few good general magazines are desirable. The following list is suggestive. It includes magazines in which high school students and teachers will be interested.

Century	$4.00
Independent	4.00
Literary digest	3.00
National geographic magazine	2.50
Outing	3.00

Popular mechanics..................$1.50

Review of reviews (American)..........3.00

Scientific American..................4.00

Scribner's..........................3.00

Survey..............................3.00

World's work........................3.00

Youth's companion..................2.00

Reader's guide. Quarterly cumulations..4.00

(This will index the magazines taken in the library)

Supplies

Condensed accession book: $1.00.

Library of Congress Printed Catalog cards: 2 cents for the first card, and ½ cent each for the duplicate cards. "Printed cards solve many difficulties for the librarian."

Book Pockets (make your own): plain slip of manila paper 3¼ × 4¾ cost 40 cents a 1000 and a Bristol card 2 × 5 inches cost $1.50 a 1000.

Sheboygan chairs (12 to a table): $2.00 each.

Librarian's flat-top desk and swivel chair: $25.00.

Size rule with scale for book sizes: 20 cents.

Classification. Dewey decimal classification. Abridged. Cloth: $1.50.

Card catalog. 4 tray catalog case: $8.00.

Catalog cards and shelf list cards. (6000). If cards are to be written by hand get "Ruled for pen" cards. If typewritten, get unruled cards. Get best grade of cards which will cost from $1.75 to $3.00 a 1000.

Buff bristol guide cards. 200 in thirds. Same size as catalog cards. 50 cents per 100.

Book pockets 2000. Printed with rules for borrowers $2.50 to $4.00 a 1000.

Book cards or charging cards. Ruled. 75 cents to $1.25 a 1000.

Charging tray 55 cents.

Date guides, 1-31 in buff bristol (one set) 35 cents.

Band dater and ink pad, about 75 cents.

Gummed labels, plain white. 25 cents to 30 cents a box, containing 1000.

India ink for marking labels. 25 cents a bottle.

Rubber stamp having name of the library. 50 cents.

White shellac, 10 cents.

Ammonia 5 cents.

A library of 10,000 volumes will cost $12,500.
—William Frederick Poole (U.S. Commissioner
of Education), 1876

☆ ☆ ☆

The present school law [Illinois] provides for the purchase of libraries and apparatus from the school funds remaining after all necessary expenses are paid, no provisions being made for appropriations for library purposes in making up the estimates. —*Public Libraries*, 1897

☆ ☆ ☆

In one place in the woods of Wisconsin an enthusiastic teacher, who could get no money for books, asked her pupils to bring an egg each day, and soon had enough to realize $1.50, which she expended for books.
—L. D. Harvey, 1899

The book fund, at the present prices,
should be $1.00 a term, per student.
— *School Library Service*, 1923

(*Public Libraries*. Vol. 6. 1901)

A library dependent upon charity for its existence is likely to be left to
live upon good wishes only.   — Virginia Lynch, 1924

☆ ☆ ☆

Beginning with this year every board of directors of a one-room rural
school should annually include in the budget at least $40 for a library. I am
enclosing a list of books which are to be bought for the library this year. The
approximate cost is $40. Larger districts and others desiring to spend more
for this purpose may obtain supplementary lists from this office. Provision
should be made for the proper care of the library. Each year new lists of
books to be added will be sent to the clerk.
— In a letter from the Office of the County Superintendent
of Common Schools, Vancouver, Washington, 1928

We are most unfortunate in that our Board of Education appropriates no fund for new books or library equipment. They pay the librarian's salary, but the school itself must maintain the library.... Funds have been raised for several years by giving operettas.　　　　　—Mary T. Leiper, 1926

IN SEARCH OF A BUDGET

It is a very modest estimate that puts the necessary per capita appropriation at $2.00 or more per pupil for the school of less than one hundred enrollment as against 75 cents per pupil for the large school.

—*High School Libraries in Illinois*, 1931

☆ ☆ ☆

In general $3.00 a year per pupil will buy one new book a year per pupil and pay for the binding and processing supplies.

—*Handbook on Elementary School Libraries*, 1953

BUDGET LEGACY OF THE '80's

During Title IV-B

Let the local level decide...

After Title IV-B

Selection and Censorship

Thank God there are no free schools or printing ... for learning has brought disobedience and heresy into the world. — Sir William Berkley, 1667

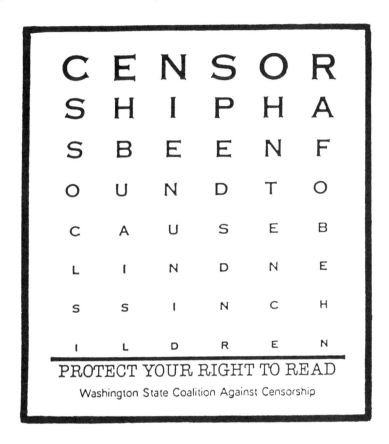

Responses from county school superintendents in the state of Michigan, 1897:

Q. To what extent is the teacher consulted in the selection of library books, and how efficiently can she advise from a knowledge of the books and the needs of the patrons and pupils?

- The teacher is not in any way consulted; could not give intelligent advice if she were.

- It is the exception rather than the rule.

- Teachers will not take the trouble to do so.

- Teachers are seldom consulted; their knowledge is too limited to be of value if they were.

- Teachers abuse the library by giving upper-form books to lower-form pupils.

I inherited a library in 1982 with the following subject card:

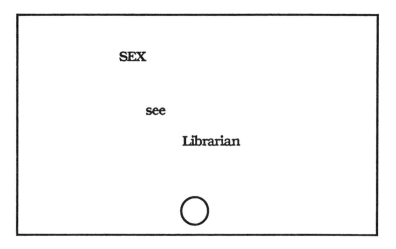

— Julianne Orlando

Librarians Take a Stand against Bad Books
"What Shall Libraries Do about Bad Books"
(Responses from library leaders, 1908)

NEW YORK PUBLIC LIBRARY

We have no hard and fast rules in the Circulation Department of the New York Public Library that enable us to tell at a glance, or at a reading, what books should be barred from use on account of immoral tendency or of indecency. Each case is treated on its own merits, and it is unnecessary to say that we do not purchase any books that appear to us to be either immoral or so indecent that they are unfit to be circulated among the general public.

— Arthur E. Bostwick

NEW BEDFORD, MASS., PUBLIC LIBRARY

That books which are questionable in morals or suggestive and indecent in tone should be excluded from libraries must be assumed. That library officials are careful in excluding books which they deem at all harmful to the morals of the community is also beyond question.

With most libraries I should say that the tendency was rather to err on the side of overrestriction, than by a laxity in admitting such books.

... there is a feeling among parents of the American Youth that their morals should be largely left to the guidance of the teachers while in school, and the Choice of books left to the library officials, who with the teachers are unofficially constituted *custodes morum*. But emphatically I believe that the salvation of the child depends on the parent rather than on the state.

— George H. Tripp

NEWARK FREE PUBLIC LIBRARY

A few books which are nasty according to present-day notions are placed on restricted shelves and are issued to adults only; they are given unhesitantingly to such adults as ask for them.

— Sara Cleveland Van de Carr

ATLANTA, CARNEGIE LIBRARY

It was recently brought to my attention that a certain set of books not suitable for unrestricted circulation was being largely read by high-school boys and girls. These books were passed from one to another, the whole set being constantly in circulation. These works of fiction, written by one of the continental authors, were classified as literature, with the idea that this would restrict their use. After discovering their unprecedented popularity the books were removed from the shelves, and will finally be discarded.

This brings me to say what I really feel about books of this class — that the public library is not the place for them. There are comparatively few readers who take these books from the library for study, and those who wish them for such a purpose can purchase them.

— Julia T. Rankin

CLEVELAND PUBLIC LIBRARY

Fiction and any other questionable literature is ordered on approval, read and reported on by one or more persons on the volunteer reading committee or on the library staff; reviews of the books are also looked up and compared. If the moral tone of the book is low, it is excluded from the library, unless it has some distinct merits, literary or other, which warrant keeping one copy as a restricted book at the main library. Restricted books are under the direct supervision of the head of the department, to whom application for such books must be made; they are loaned to the branches only by request through the branch librarian, and their use is confined to readers of mature judgment. The greatest safeguard against interest in bad literature is of course a cultivation of the good, hence we aim to supply the best clean fiction unstintingly, duplicating it very largely.

— William Howard Brett

TRAVELING LIBRARY DEPARTMENT, WISCONSIN LIBRARY COMMISSION

This is the day of "exotic," "erotic," and "tommy-rotic" literature and the problem of selection is becoming increasingly difficult. Out of forty recent titles of fiction, taken at random from publishers' lists, there were just two of a happy, wholesome nature that came up to the standard for traveling libraries. We realize that the standard of such libraries sent to rural communities is much higher than for the average city library, as country dwellers, praise be, will not "stand for" the sort of thing read by many city borrowers ... and if a work by a modern degenerate should creep into a travelling library, those in charge of the system would hear from it in no uncertain terms.

— Lute E. Stearns

PORTLAND, WIS., LIBRARY
ASSOCIATION OF PORTLAND

This being an open shelf library, all these novels of doubtful moral teaching, together with certain classics, some few medical books, etc., are kept under lock and key in the librarians office and marked with a "Minor label" plate. The catalog cards show no location and the small collection is held in mind without difficulty by the assistant. The young people seldom discover the existence of this forbidden fruit; they consult the catalog, and then finding the book missing from the shelves conclude that it is out in circulation. A few library-wise women with morbid tastes yearn for a sight of the "shut up shelves," but in vain, for no one is allowed to go to these shelves; books must be requested from the catalog.   —Mary Frances Isom

GRAND RAPIDS PUBLIC LIBRARY

I understand that there are libraries where practically all books in favor of socialism are tabooed, and others where all published writings of Mr. Bryan, until recent years, were denied a place on the shelves. In fact, to the minds of certain persons, any book which is a criticism of, or whose purpose is to change, the present social order is regarded as unwholesome, if not immoral, and therefore should have no place on library shelves, inasmuch as it is likely to awaken or engender class strife. To deal with books of this character it seems to me is not a difficult problem at all. Representatives of all shades of views on social, economic, and religious questions should have a place on library shelves.   —Samuel H. Ranck

How to Make a Moral Selection

What is an immoral novel ... just how does a novel accomplish our undoing?

1. The book may make a direct appeal to our lower nature....

2. The novel harms us when it confuses right and wrong. The book which does this may be quite respectable, it may contain nothing obviously offensive and yet it may be an immoral book....

3. A book may neither appeal to our worse selves, nor fail to distinguish good from evil, and may yet be so *untrue to life* as to be immoral.

—"What Makes a Novel Immoral?," *New York Libraries*, 1908

Book Selection (and Deselection)

Some of the Most Significant Finds

1. The policy of encouraging by state aid the purchase of books from a selected list seems justified, for the books read are chiefly from the school libraries and are of good quality.

2. Unsuitable books, although the exception, are in evidence and are obtained outside of the school-room. There is a great dearth of children's books of any kind in the home.

3. Boys read fewer but better books than girls. The majority of rural children read very few books and some none at all.

4. Older boys and girls read books that are too simple, "The Dutch Twins" and "Little Black Sambo" being read in every grade. This may be due to a lack of mechanical ability or the development of a taste for the best books.

5. Teachers must read more children's books to be able to guide the home reading and to make selections of informational material. More books on history, geography and travel for first reading, are needed. Fiction for older pupils now predominates.

(From a study of Minnesota's rural elementary school libraries, circa 1926)

Every precaution should be taken that school libraries shall consist of well-selected books. The achievement of this result will be greatly facilitated if a list of books is issued by the state from which list books must be selected in order to entitle school districts to special library aid. It is gratifying to be able to say that already twenty-six of the states issue lists of books for school libraries, some annually, some biennially, and others at longer intervals.
— *Rural School Libraries: Their Needs and Possibilities*, 1913

☆ ☆ ☆

Every district should have a dictionary, usually an unabridged one of recent date. In case of a district of not more than ten thousand dollars assessed valuation, or one having only a very few and very young pupils, such a dictionary as *Webster's Collegiate*, which may be had for three dollars, would answer very well. A school of considerable size containing some children well advanced should have an encyclopedia if the district can afford it. A fairly good encyclopedia of six volumes can be had now for $18. It should be borne in mind, however, that neither a dictionary nor an encyclopedia will be of very great value unless the teacher instructs the pupils in its use. — *University of the State of New York Bulletin*, No. 539, 1913

Book Selection:

It is an easy matter to select the first hundred books for a school library as the law requires them to be selected from the list published by the Superintendent of Public Instruction of the State.

— *A Library Primer for High Schools*, 1917

☆ ☆ ☆

Series written for girls are the poorest of their kind. It is hardly an exaggeration to say that almost all fiction written for girls is entirely hopeless from either the literary or ethical standpoint. The heroines are impossibly rich, or good, or bright, or beautiful. Most of the long series for girls reek with snobbishness and admiration for wealth, and when the remarkable heroine is not slangy or obsessed with worldly ideas, she is impossibly goody-goody, with a tendency to reform her parents and other people within her reach. Even the books which present fairly human characters and in which the atmosphere is wholesome, are insipid and have nothing special to recommend them. — *The Children's Library: A Dynamic Factor in Education*, 1917

☆ ☆ ☆

The remark is attributed to George Bancroft, that the history of all Europe must yet be written from an American standpoint in order that we may obtain correct views of the events on that continent. We should act upon the suggestions of that remark in making lists of books for our school libraries. — Charles Howard Shinn, 1890

☆ ☆ ☆

I was once principal of a grammar school in a large town, and I had the pleasure of burning a copy of one of G. M. Reynold's novels, and a well-thumbed edition of the *Pirate's Own*. — Charles Howard Shinn, 1890

☆ ☆ ☆

The underlying principle of my own selection of books, for a library which is essentially for the people, is that books that spread truth concerning normal, wholesome conditions may be safely bought, however plain-spoken. While on the other hand, books which treat of morbid, diseased conditions of the individual man, or of society at large, are intended for the student of special subjects. Such are bought only after due consideration of the just relation of the comparative rights of the students and general readers. — Theresa H. West, 1895

☆ ☆ ☆

It is for the girls, however, that we would make a special plea; so much pain is often taken to interest boys in biography, history, travel, and science, but the girl who wants a book (and she is more prone than her brother to leave the selection of her books to another's judgement) is given a "pretty story," and she goes on reading the "pretty story," until the first thing you know she is in the ranks of those who read nothing but the silly, the sentimental, and the sensational novels. — Linda A. Eastman, 1896

School libraries should contain an abundance of what may be called collateral reading, relating to every part of the curriculum. When a volume is found to be both instructive and specially interesting, duplicate it. More is accomplished by five copies of a good book that finds its own readers than by ten good books that must be helped to an audience.   —G. T. Little, 1896

☆ ☆ ☆

Don't admit a book into the children's department of your library without careful examination. Scrutinize new authors critically and avoid those whose language and theme have a swagger not calculated to raise the standard of a child's imagination.   —L. E. Stearns, 1896

☆ ☆ ☆

I should, in a district school library, avoid theoretic and controversial reading for teachers who are not likely to go pretty thoroughly into study of the questions involved, and select such writings as will kindle enthusiasm for the work and give sensible suggestions, without raising complex questions.
—Milicent W. Shinn, 1896

☆ ☆ ☆

As a general thing I do not believe in books written for children. Most seem to be a fatal mistake, enfeebling to young minds ... I am not sure but it would be a gain if all the so-called children's books were destroyed, and the children depended altogether on what we call adult literature.
—Charles Dudley Warner, 1896

☆ ☆ ☆

The library has no right to set itself up as a censor of public morals, forbidding men to read anything.   —W. R. Eastman, 1897

☆ ☆ ☆

There is not need for a great variety, but for several copies of only the best in different departments of literature.   —Mary E. Sargent, 1901

☆ ☆ ☆

In the matter of books, experience has proved that it is a serious mistake to depend upon donations.   —*Public Libraries*, 1901

☆ ☆ ☆

Our literature is menaced both from below and from above. Books that distinctly commend what is wrong, that teach how to sin and tell how pleasant sin is, sometimes with and sometimes without the added sauce of impropriety, are increasingly popular, tempting the author to imitate them, the publishers to produce, the booksellers to exploit. Thank heaven they do not tempt the librarian. Here at last is a purveyor of books who has no interest in distributing what is not clean, honest, and true. The librarian may, if he will—and he does—say to this menacing tide, "Thus far shalt thou go and no farther."   —Arthur E. Bostwick, 1908

"Some are born great; some achieve greatness; some have greatness thrust upon them." It is in this last way that the librarian has become a censor of literature. Originally the custodian of volumes placed in his care by others, he has ended by becoming in these latter days much else, including a selector and distributor.... As the library's audience becomes larger, as its educational functions spread and are brought to bear on more and more of the young and immature, the duty of sifting its material becomes more imperative. —Arthur E. Bostwick, 1908

☆ ☆ ☆

It may be fatal to a patient to let him know how ill he is. And may it not also be injurious to a young man or a young woman to expose the amount of evil that really lies before them in this world? —Arthur E. Bostwick, 1908

☆ ☆ ☆

The subject has interested me ever since a schoolmate of mine tried to run away to the West to fight Indians. When he was captured and brought back it was given out that he had been misled by dime novels. His parents probably liked to blame dime novels for what was really the result of their own neglect. Those of us who knew him, knew that he never read dime novels at all. He didn't read anything—he was too stupid. There were some books, however, responsible for his outbreak, and they were: *Colburn's Arithmetic*, *Harper's School Geography*, *The Fourth Reader*, and *Somebody's Speller*. I have never heard of any of *them* denounced as immoral, but their influence on that occasion was exactly that which is so often attributed and falsely attributed, to dime novels. —E. L. Pearson, 1911

☆ ☆ ☆

Books are probably among the secondary
moral influences, perhaps far down on the
list. —Sophy H. Powell, 1917

☆ ☆ ☆

All the ills from which America suffers can be tracked back to the teaching of evolution. It would be better to destroy every other book ever written, and save just the first three verses of Genesis. —William Jennings Bryan, 1924

☆ ☆ ☆

Books are not good fuel.... In the days when heretical books were burned, it was necessary to place them on large wooden stages, and after all the pains taken to demolish them, considerable readable masses were sometimes found in the embers; whence it was supposed that the devil, conversant in fire and its effects, gave them his special protection. In the end it was found easier and cheaper to burn the heretics themselves than their books. —W. G. Clifford, 1926

A third problem which belongs peculiarly to the school library is that of trashy, obscene and worthless literature. The newsstands of many cities literally reek with magazines and books that thrive on the morbidity of youth. The distribution of such literature should be prohibited. It means much to the library cause for librarians to be active in such movements.

—Joy Elmer Morgan, 1926

☆ ☆ ☆

Mark Twain's reply to librarian, Asa Don Dickinson, concerning the banning of *Huckleberry Finn* in children's rooms on the grounds that "Huck not only itched but scratched, and that he said sweat when he should have said perspiration":

It always distresses me when I find that boys and girls have been allowed access to ... [*Tom Sawyer* and *Huckleberry Finn*]. The mind that became soiled in youth can never again be washed clean.... To this day I cherish an unappeasable bitterness against the unfaithful guardians of my young life, who not only permitted but compelled me to read an unexpurgated Bible through before I was 15.

—*Wilson Bulletin*, 1936

☆ ☆ ☆

Where books are burned, human beings will be burned too.
—Heinrich Heine

☆ ☆ ☆

Censorship reflects a society's lack of confidence in itself. It is hallmark of an authoritarian regime. —Justice Potter Stewart

☆ ☆ ☆

The fact is that censorship always defeats its own purpose, for it creates, in the end, the kind of society that is incapable of exercising real discretion.... In the long run it will create a generation incapable of appreciating the difference between independence of thought and subservience.

—Henry Steele Commager

Once a government is committed to the principle of silencing the voice of opposition, it has only one way to go, and that is down the path of increasingly repressive measures, until it becomes a source of terror to all its citizens and creates a country where everyone lives in fear.
— Harry S. Truman

We all know books burn—yet we have the greater knowledge that books cannot be killed by fire. People die, but books never die.... No man and no force can put thought in a concentration camp forever.... Books are weapons ... make them weapons for man's freedom.
— Franklin Delano Roosevelt

☆ ☆ ☆

If this nation is to be wise as well as strong, if we are to achieve our destiny, then we need more new ideas for more wise men reading more good books in more public libraries. These libraries should be open to all—except the censor. We must know all the facts and hear all the alternatives and listen to all the criticisms. Let us welcome controversial books and controversial authors. For the Bill of Rights is the guardian of our security as well as our liberty.
— John F. Kennedy

Free speech, rather than being the enemy, is a long-tested and worthy ally. To deny free speech in order to engineer social change in the name of accomplishing a greater good for one sector of our society erodes the freedoms of all and, as such, threatens tyranny and injustice for those subjected to the rule of such laws.

— *American Booksellers Association, Inc.*
et al. v. William H. Hudnut III, 1984

☆ ☆ ☆

In the long run of history, the censor and the inquisitor have always lost. The only sure weapon against bad ideas is better ideas. The source of better ideas is wisdom. — Alfred Whitney Griswold

☆ ☆ ☆

Censors only read a book with great difficulty, moving their lips as they puzzle out each syllable, when somebody tells them that the book is unfit to read. — Robertson Davies

☆ ☆ ☆

A censor is a expert in cutting remarks. A censor is a man who knows more than you ought to. — Laurence J. Peter

☆ ☆ ☆

Words in a book can never be harmful, period. To adults or to minors. — Bernie Rath

☆ ☆ ☆

Censorship is based on the notion that if people can be kept ignorant, they can be kept pure. — Stephen Robinson

☆ ☆ ☆

Everyone wants to protect the children. The problem is, they're going to be so protected they won't be able to function in the year 2000. — Judith Krug

☆ ☆ ☆

I think it is not American to censor. Aside from the very grave legal factors surrounding the issue of freedom of access to library materials, there is one devastating *practical* matter involved. Whenever an individual, or group, or board decides to become the arbiter of community tastes or morals and orders the removal of a book from a collection, what will happen when the next complaint comes in, and the next one, and the one after that? Will you pick and choose on the basis of *who* made the complaint? If you do, then you'll be judging people and their characters and their standing in the community as well as judging books.

— Duane Meyers. Reprinted by permission. Voice of Youth
Advocates/Scarecrow Press. "Learning to Live,"
VOYA, June 1988.

"I just knew that your library would want these. I certainly can't bring myself to throw them away."

We call it "book selecting" because we buy so few books.
— Robert L. Balliot

☆ ☆ ☆

Donations to the Bothell High School library collection are always welcome. Sometimes we get an explanatory note along with them. Along with one book was the accompanying, "Can you use this book? It has some sex affairs in it."
— Marianne Gregersen

☆ ☆ ☆

The *Book of Lists #1* was challenged at our school as not being suitable reference material for those with Christian values. When asked if she had read the book in its entirety, the parent replied, "Yes." In response to whether the book had *any* redeeming values, she replied vehemently, "None at all!"

The book contains, among other lists, outstanding Medal of Honor winners, the best American children's books of the past 200 years, and the Lord Thy God's 10 Commandments.
— Lee King

☆ ☆ ☆

Sign on a media specialist's desk: "This library has something to offend everyone."
— Roberta Margo

At a public forum concerning the removal of a certain book from a school collection, a woman complained about the lack of books on topics such as "... cooking, sewing, diaphragming sentences...."

—Nancy Motomatsu

☆ ☆ ☆

A parent challenging Zilpha Snyder's *Headless Cupid* because of seance, occult, and witchcraft references, was horrified to learn that our school system must call our Christmas concerts "Winter Concerts," and use only candy canes instead of angels and stars in order not to offend our Jewish community. However, it made my point that each religion or interest group has legitimate concerns. —Karen K. Niemeyer

A parent complained to the principal about a book in our elementary library. The parent believed the book was satanic. Naturally, the parent came to see me on Halloween when I was dressed as a witch, just after a teacher hung a little "devil" around me. —Pat Bowers

Censors view the library media specialist

Library media specialists view the censor

Books and Authors

Some books are to be tasted, others to be swallowed, and some few to be chewed and digested.   —Francis Bacon

☆ ☆ ☆

He who has books is happy; he who does not need any is happier.   —Chinese proverb

☆ ☆ ☆

A teacher should not strike his pupil with a book, and the student should not ward off a blow with a book. A teacher should not pound on a book in anger. Do not use a book to protect yourself against the sun or smoke. Do not use it to hide something under it. Do not keep books together with food lest mice be lured by the food nibble at the books. If a book does not close easily, do not force it together with your knees.   —Hebrew proverb

☆ ☆ ☆

"What is the use of a book," thought Alice, "without pictures or conversations?"
                          —Lewis Carroll

☆ ☆ ☆

If you would not be forgotten, as soon as you are dead and rotten, either write things worth reading, or do things worth the writing.
                          —Benjamin Franklin, 1738

☆ ☆ ☆

Books are the quietest and most constant of friends; they are the most accessible and wisest of counsellors, and the most patient of teachers.
                          —Charles William Eliot, 1896

☆ ☆ ☆

Magazines all too frequently lead to books and should be regarded by the prudent as the heavy petting of literature.   —Fran Lebowitz

☆ ☆ ☆

We fancy that any real child might be more puzzled than enchanted by this stiff, overwrought story.
                          —Review of *Alice's Adventures in Wonderland*,
                          in *Children's Books*, 1865

☆ ☆ ☆

A classic is something that everybody wants to have read and nobody wants to read.   —Mark Twain

A hundred years from now it is very likely that [of all of Mark Twain's works] *The Jumping Frog* alone will be remembered.
—Harry Thurston Peck, 1901

☆ ☆ ☆

American fiction ..., while it may not be national, and may not be great, it will have at least the negative virtue of being clean.   —Bliss Perry, 1902

☆ ☆ ☆

When I am dead, I hope it may be said:
His sins were scarlet, but his books were read.
—Hilaire Belloc

☆ ☆ ☆

In order to make sure that children like what we think they ought to like, we force upon them our own ready-made opinions about the books which every man who would call himself educated should read. —Sophy H. Powell

☆ ☆ ☆

It is a great thing to start life with a small number of really good books which are your very own.   —Sir Arthur Conan Doyle

☆ ☆ ☆

The love of books is a love which requires neither justification, apology, nor defense.   —J. A. Langford

☆ ☆ ☆

I shall always have a strong preference for cheap books myself, even if they did not pay; all my little friends happen to be shilling people. I do dislike the modern fashion of giving children heaps of expensive things which they don't look at twice.   —Beatrix Potter

☆ ☆ ☆

When I have something I want to say that's too difficult for most adults, I'll have a young protagonist and I'll write it for kids. They haven't closed their doors to new ideas yet.   —Madeleine L'Engle

☆ ☆ ☆

A kid is a guy I never write down to. He's interested in what I say if I make it interesting. He is also the last container of a sense of humor, which disappears as he gets older, and he laughs only according to the way the boss, society, politics, or race, want him to. Then he becomes an adult. And an adult is an obsolete child.   —Theodore Geisel, a.k.a. Dr. Seuss

Illustrated editions and beautiful picture books multiply as a result of adult demand rather than desire or need of children.   —Sophy H. Powell

☆ ☆ ☆

Someone once said to a children's book editor, "In adult publishing it's dog eat dog. Is that true in children's books?" And the editor replied, "Oh, no. In children's books, it's bunny nibble bunny." I think the point is that, though we have to be a business and pay our way, in children's books we can be competitive and idealistic at the same time.   —James Giblin

☆ ☆ ☆

Any reviewer who expresses rage and loathing for a novel is preposterous. He or she is like a person who has put on full armor and attacked a hot fudge sundae.   —Kurt Vonnegut, Jr.

☆ ☆ ☆

Writing is like prostitution. First you do it for love, then you do it for just a few friends, and then you do it for the money.
     —Moliére, as quoted in *The Courant*, Centralia College

☆ ☆ ☆

All literature is gossip.
     —Truman Capote

☆ ☆ ☆

A historical romance is the only kind of
book where chastity really counts.
     —Attributed to Barbara Cartland

☆ ☆ ☆

This is not a novel to be tossed aside
lightly. It should be thrown with great force.
     —Dorothy Parker

☆ ☆ ☆

Books are good enough in their own way,
but they are a mighty bloodless substitute for
life.   —Robert Louis Stevenson

☆ ☆ ☆

People say that life is the thing, but I
prefer reading.   —Logan Pearsall Smith

☆ ☆ ☆

Get stewed: Books are a load of crap.
     —Philip Larkin

There is no such thing as an immoral
book. Books are well written, or badly
written.   —Oscar Wilde

☆ ☆ ☆

The difference between truth and fiction
is that fiction has to make sense.
—Mark Twain

☆ ☆ ☆

Nine-tenths of the existing books are nonsense, and the clever books are
the refutation of that nonsense. The greatest misfortune that ever befell man
was the invention of the printing press.   —Benjamin Disraeli

☆ ☆ ☆

At this time I had decided the only thing I was fit for was to be a writer,
and this notion rested solely on my suspicion that I would never be fit for real
work, and that writing didn't require any.   —Russell Baker

☆ ☆ ☆

Before I start to write, I always treat myself to a nice dry martini. Just
one, to give me the courage to get started. After that, I am on my own.
—E. B. White

☆ ☆ ☆

The most essential gift for a good writer
is a built-in shock-proof s—t-detector.
—Ernest Hemingway

☆ ☆ ☆

A wonderful thing about a book, in contrast to a computer screen, is
that you can take it to bed with you. You can embrace a book. You can hide
it. It becomes part of you. You own it in the best sense of the word—in the
sense that it owns you, too, if it's a great book.   —Daniel J. Boorstin

☆ ☆ ☆

It is not true that we have only one life to live; if we can read, we can live
as many more lives and as many kinds as we wish.   —S. I. Hayakawa

☆ ☆ ☆

Make your books your companions.
—The Talmud

Reading

In my opinion, however, our High School courses of study in English Literature *should begin with the authors of to-day, (American), and go back to* Chaucer instead of beginning with Chaucer and coming down to the present time.   —B. Peaslee, 1881

☆ ☆ ☆

An American child should no more be allowed to read an adverse criticism of American institutions, and of American social conditions, than he should be allowed to read an adverse criticism of his family.

—Charles Howard Shinn, 1890

☆ ☆ ☆

Even a wayfaring man can see here the duty of the school in library work. By law, the children are put under your influence in their earlier years when, if ever, they can be taught to love good books so well that all their lives thereafter they will seize on every opportunity to read them.

—Melvil Dewey, 1896

☆ ☆ ☆

As a rule, children do not need to be taught to read fiction, but by cultivating in them a taste for history, literature, natural science, etc., we may be reasonably sure that they will choose only the better class of fiction when left to themselves.   —Hannah P. James, 1896

☆ ☆ ☆

It makes no particular difference whether they read or not, unless they read what is valuable.   —Richard Jones, 1897

☆ ☆ ☆

[Concerning the reading of dime novels as a youngster] I read *Sixteen String Jack*, and *Dick Turpin*, and all of those English books, biographies of highwaymen, and quite innumerable books and story papers of similar character.... But I am obliged to confess that I am not sorry that I read that miserable stuff. I am glad I read it.   —John W. Cook, 1897

☆ ☆ ☆

Better that a small child should read
Hans Andersen than worry his little brain
over nine plus seven.

—Anonymous comment at the
NEA Conference, 1898

If one be so unfortunate as to crave demoralizing literature, he will suffer no more from the reading of it than if he were left with his own thoughts. —Elizabeth Skinner, 1899

☆ ☆ ☆

Hashed victual, especially literary hash, should be taken by goats rather than fed to children. —J. M. Greenwood, 1902

☆ ☆ ☆

Girls rarely read books calculated to fit them for domestic life or womanly vocations of any kind. —G. Stanley Hall, 1905

☆ ☆ ☆

Those who batten upon the modern novel, with its highly artificial and conventional treatment of ante-nuptial love, often treated in a somewhat risque manner, cannot possible know life. —G. Stanley Hall, 1905

☆ ☆ ☆

The maxim, "Art for art's sake," has absolutely no place in education; for there is only one standard of merit in the reading of school children, and that is its moral value. —G. Stanley Hall, 1905

☆ ☆ ☆

Artistic appreciation usually requires cultivated taste, and only the privileged class can have leisure for the full development of the trained eye and ear. Nevertheless, educators have assumed that a cultivated taste is an essential part of every child's equipment. —Sophy H. Powell, 1917

☆ ☆ ☆

I have no difficulty whatever in naming the books that I read as a child.... I very soon decided that Charles Dickens was the greatest writer who ever lived on this earth.... At the time when I was reading Dickens for myself I was being made to read at school such stuff as Milton's "Paradise Lost." I was glad that it was lost, but wished that it had been lost beyond recall....

As a writer of books it is my opinion that children, or at least young persons—are the best readers. Grown-up adults are badly damaged. They read in an inattentive way, with no real effort of mental power to fuse the picture before them in the white heat of imagination. They read and forget.... Their judgements are the standard of education and their admiration lies dead in the grave of their childhood. For real literary success let me tell a fairy story to the listening ears and wondering face of my little son of four. —Stephen B. Leacock, 1920

☆ ☆ ☆

Reading, to most people, means an ashamed way of killing time disguised under a dignified name. —Ernest Dimnet, 1928

I never was much on this book reading, for it takes 'em too long to describe the color of the eyes of all the characters. — Will Rogers, 1949

☆ ☆ ☆

The man who reads only for improvement is beyond the hope of much improvement before he begins. — Jonathan Daniels, 1956

☆ ☆ ☆

My alma mater was books, a good library.... I could spend the rest of my life reading, just satisfying my curiosity. — Malcolm X, 1964

☆ ☆ ☆

Access to interesting and informative books is one of the keys to a successful reading program. As important as an adequate collection of books is a librarian who encourages wide reading and helps match books to children. — *Becoming a Nation of Readers*, National Academy of Education, Commission on Reading, 1986

☆ ☆ ☆

There is no shortage of wonderful writers. What we lack is a dependable mass of readers.... I propose that every person out of work be required to submit a book report before he or she gets his or her welfare check.
— Kurt Vonnegut, Jr.

People in general do not willingly read, if they can have anything else to amuse them.   —Samuel Johnson

☆ ☆ ☆

Books have led some to learning and others to madness.   —Petrarch

Many husbands find it difficult to keep their wives from reading, and there are even some who contend that reading has this advantage, that at least they know what their wives are doing.   —Honoré de Balzac

☆ ☆ ☆

I read my eyes out and can't read half enough.... The more one reads the more one sees we have to read.   —John Adams

☆ ☆ ☆

The man who does not read good books has not advantage over the man who can't read them.   —Mark Twain

☆ ☆ ☆

I strongly suspect that we would have many more readers than we have, and many fewer reading problems, if for all children under the age of 10 or even 12 reading were made illegal.   —John Holt

☆ ☆ ☆

Reading is one of our bad habits.... We read, most of the time, not because we wish to instruct ourselves, not because we long to have our feelings touched and our imagination fired, but ... because we have time to spare.   —Aldous Huxley

☆ ☆ ☆

I find that the only thing that really stands up, better than gambling, better than booze, better than women, is reading.   —Mario Puzo

There are some people who read too much.... I know some who are constantly drunk on books, as other men are drunk on whiskey or religion. They wander through this most diverting and stimulating of worlds in a haze, seeing nothing and hearing nothing.

—H. L. Mencken

☆ ☆ ☆

I'm reading *Why Women Love Men Who Leave Women Who Cling to Men Who Fear Commitment Who Can't Talk to Women Who Love Too Much!*

This will never be a civilized country until we expend more money for books than we do for chewing gum.

—Attributed to Elbert Hubbard

Next to hugging your child, reading aloud is probably the longest-lasting experience that you can put into your child's life. You will savor it long after they have grown up. Reading aloud is important for all the reasons that talking to children is important — to inspire them, to guide them, to educate them, to bond with them and to communicate your feelings, hopes and fears. You are giving children a piece of your mind and a piece of your time.

— Jim Trelease

"Got anything light and fun to read, like V. C. Andrews or Stephen King?"

How to Induce School Reading
1897

We of the public schools have a few perplexing characters to deal with, who, like the poor, are always with us. We have the child who has never read a book, and we know not how to reach his understanding. He is only capable of continuing the old-time drill, The cat is on the mat. Can the cat trot? Yes, the cat can trot. And that child is a sure candidate to trot all his life in a half bushel.

We have the child who has been compelled by unwise parents, to read unseasoned literature, either above or beneath his taste, so that the work of creating a hunger for reading has to be done over from the beginning, and a discouraging task it is. None but a real teacher can possibly succeed.

Then we have the boy who has read dime novels and N.Y. Ledger stories. He can only be sent to an asylum for incurables.

Then we encounter the omnivorous readers of Oliver Optic and Henty, whose disease is congestion. I can not believe that the apparent stupidity of these children is from reading as to quantity. They may lie down and read in an unhealthy position, or they use improper hours. They form an inordinate taste for one author and style and, like the Hindoo who gazes at one object and sits in one position until he becomes absorbed into Brahama or Buddha, they enter upon an absorbed, dreamy plane, so that the teacher must throw a book or ruler at them to wake them when attention is called....

The first attempts at juvenile literature of more than twenty years ago were found in Sunday School libraries. And Sunday School books were a snare and a delusion, a conglomeration of exaggeration in which the prominent characters were three bears and a balk head....

In our schools ... [we teach] historical stories from the fourth grade up, including also some works of Irving, Hawthorne, Whittier, Lowell, Longfellow, Ruskin. Typical among these works are Grandfather's chair, King of the Golden River, Evangeline, Thanatopsis, Webster's speech and Hayne's reply, Burke's conciliation, Shakespeare's Julius Caesar and Merchant of Venice. Ninety sets are now in our course, so that each pupil with us eight years, reads at least ninety complete works of the world's best literature and this under guidance of his teacher....

Another exercise is followed in all the grades. One day a week the pupil tells before the class in choice language a fable or legend, and most of these stories are drawn from our poetical literature, such stories as The Stolen Necklace in Evangeline, or Abou Ben Adhem or the Blind Men and the Elephant, Hiawatha and pearl Feather, The Skeleton in Armor, etc. The Iliad and Odyssey, the Eddas, Siegfried, Roland and King Arthur are quite familiar to our twelve-year-old boys and girls.

Clean Books in the Children's Room

THIS IS A NEW BOOK
DO NOT HANDLE IT UNLESS
YOUR HANDS ARE CLEAN

Is printed in attractive type, on a blue label and tipped on page one, of every new volume in the Children's Department at the Lincoln Library, Springfield, Illinois.

On a reading table near the loan desk is a register also wearing a label of blue. This label bears an inscription whose form is changed frequently, that the story may not become old, but always requiring the pledge: "I promise to keep this new book clean and fresh or pay all damages."

Soap and paper towels are kept at the desk for the soiled hands "just from work or play" and the children are encouraged to feel it a virtue rather than a disgrace to make frequent use of both, before selecting their books.

As each new volume is charged, a paper jacket is slipped on, or laid on the book and the child told to read the pledge and register his name. Frequently the reply is "I've signed a'ready!" and often these little keepers of clean books initiate new members into the rules of the game, for us.

When a volume has passed the point of being fresh and new, the label is removed and the child's signature is no longer required.

Records of the circulation of some of the most popular titles, show their condition to be fresh and readable twice as long as when the children were reminded and not obligated to be thoughtful in the care of books.

Lang's "Colored books," Pinocchio, and Grimm's Household tales, especial favorites of our little new Americans, whose only place of safekeeping from baby fingers, is on the kitchen cabinet or under the bed, are not decorated with nearly so many culinary earmarks or torn leaves, since Rosie and Angelo have "signed to keep 'em clean."   — *Illinois Librarian*, April 4, 1919

PART 3   TECHNOLOGY IN THE LIBRARY

Those Blessed and Blasted Machines

The latest agent has just gone out the door and I am beginning to detest typewriter agents and salesmen. I like men and machines well enough, and I have good digestion and ought to be with fair mind and without bias.

The machine man attempts to talk — to induce hypnosis and to sell the machine before the subject awakes from the trance. He has just been here for two hours. If you see him don't let him in.   — Joseph F. Daniels, 1901

THE NEW
=== No. 2 ===
HAMMOND TYPE-WRITER

WORK IN SIGHT

THIS WILL INTEREST YOU

For Card Index Work

The Hammond Typewriter

Takes the Index Card flat, holds it flat, prints it flat, and finally delivers it flat, and all this without "attachments" of any sort.

The Hammond has a special library type, and furthermore, prints in any language, style of type or co'or of ink on the same machine.

Hammond Typewriter Black Record Ribbons have been tested by United States Government chemists, and have been pronounced "undoubtedly permanent."

IF YOU ARE A LIBRARIAN

THE **HAMMOND TYPEWRITER COMPANY**

Factory, 69th to 70th Streets, East River,

NEW YORK, U. S. A.

Branches in Principal Cities.
Representatives Everywhere.

WORK IN SIGHT

79

The dime and nickel novel publisher is suffering from the competition of the motion picture theaters.   Sophy H. Powell, 1917

☆ ☆ ☆

While theoretically and technically television may be feasible, commercially and financially I consider it an impossibility, a development of which we need waste little time dreaming.   — Lee De Forest, 1926

☆ ☆ ☆

In addition to books, challenging new materials are becoming an important part of library resources. Some new audio-visual aids for learning are 16mm films, film-strips, slides, museum objects, radio programs....
— *Schools and Public Libraries Working Together*
in School Library Service, 1941

Library Bureau patented steel stack, showing special lighting device.

Library Bureau patent diamond frame steel stacks are the most adjustable, indestructible, ornamental and adaptable; well lighted and ventilated. Hundreds of libraries and offices use them. Illustrated descriptive catalog, designs and estimates, sent on application.

Technology brings light to the stacks!   (*Public Libraries.* Vol. 6. 1901)

Perhaps one of the reasons why we do not feel librarians are qualified and why the library has not developed into a material center is because the school librarian cannot handle the mechanical end of it. Most librarians are women.   —*Avenues and Vistas for Bringing Library Materials to Children and Young People*, 1948

☆ ☆ ☆

I have anticipated [radio's] complete disappearance—confident that the unfortunate people, who must not subdue themselves to "listening in," will soon find a better pastime for their leisure.   —H. G. Wells

☆ ☆ ☆

Any sufficiently advanced technology is indistinguishable from magic.
           —Arthur Clarke

☆ ☆ ☆

This may be the last generation of writers; in the future, everything may be taped.   —Attributed to Clive Barnes

☆ ☆ ☆

Video won't be able to hold onto any market it captures after the first six months. People will soon get tired of staring at a plywood box every night.
           —Attributed to Darryl F. Zanuck

☆ ☆ ☆

Television is: The literature of the illiterate.
           —Lee Loevinger

☆ ☆ ☆

Television—a medium. So called because it is neither rare nor well done.   —Ernie Kovacs

☆ ☆ ☆

I must say I find television very educational. The minute somebody turns it on, I go to the library and read a good book.   —Groucho Marx

☆ ☆ ☆

If you read a lot of books, you're considered well-read. But if you watch a lot of TV, you're not considered well-viewed.   —Lily Tomlin

☆ ☆ ☆

A book is what they make a movie out of for television.   —Leonard Louis Levinson

Woe is me ... because less than 3 percent of you people read books! Because less than 15 percent of you read newspapers! Because the only truth you know is what you get over this tube.　　　　— Peter Finch in *Network*

☆ ☆ ☆

If there is any one single weapon for countering the impact of television in a way that scores points for schooling, it is by helping your child get used to going to the library.　　　　— Gene I. Maeroff

☆ ☆ ☆

You can be a winner [at video games] even though you are illiterate. [Today's youth] can go from home to the shopping mall and play a video game at each end.　　　　— Richard Peck

☆ ☆ ☆

Selling technology to schools is a very difficult process. It requires what is called in the private sector a "dual sell." You must sell it to the administrator (top) and to teachers (bottom). It takes very different information to sell each.　　　　— Bob Hughes

☆ ☆ ☆

Using technology in schools today is the same as Horace Mann and Andrew Carnegie making the basic tools of literacy available to students.

— Al Rogers

☆ ☆ ☆

We must better account for individual differences within our schools. Technology can help us do this.　　　　— Albert Shanker

☆ ☆ ☆

When we finally shall have established that *media* means all kinds of formats, from books to microcomputer programs, and whatever, I hope we can return to basics and call ourselves librarians and the places where we work libraries.　　　　— Mary Virginia Gaver

☆ ☆ ☆

Technology in libraries is often the tail wagging the dog when it really should be the tongue easing the curriculum down.　　　　— Blanche Woolls

☆ ☆ ☆

The cheerleading skirts finally arrived just before the girls had to perform in them for the first time. They were so wrinkled from shipping, but there was no time to take them home and iron the pleats. The girls were desperate. Then I had an idea. Moments before the cheerleaders' performance we were in the library ironing their pleats on the dry-mount press! Naturally, I made the girls take them off before I pressed them.

— Judi Radtke

[Concerning technology] If it's worth doing,
it's worth doing badly—for a while.
—Bob Hughes

☆ ☆ ☆

An administrator made sure to reserve a Kodak™ slide projector for a presentation he was going to make that evening. He told me that the Kodak™ machines were the only brand with which he was quite familiar.

The next morning he was upset with me for not including the power cord. The model he was so "familiar" with stores the cord in a compartment underneath the machine. —L. A. P.

☆ ☆ ☆

A sign found in the bottom of a file cabinet in a 1957 school has now been laminated to hang in my darkroom. —Karen K. Niemeyer

DARKROOM

Please keep the door closed.

If the door is opened, all the

dark leaks out.

Mr. Miller the A.V. man and I were fixing the laminator. Mr. Miller leaned over to fix something as I turned the machine on to straighten the laminating film.

Just like a wringer washing machine, the laminator grabbed onto Mr. Miller's tie! The tie was nearly laminated, and Mr. Miller nearly choked. He had to take his tie off, and we had to take the machine apart. — Roberta Margo

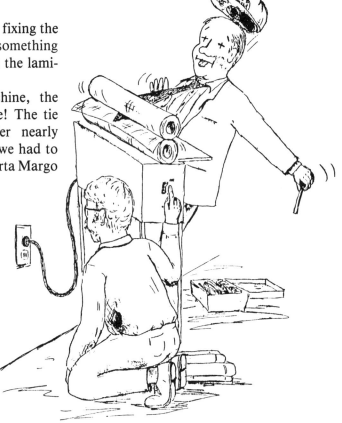

The library's photoduplicator didn't work, and as with other A.V. items, I decided to check it out and try to fix it.

I opened it up. I checked for misfeeds here, Canadian coins there. The paper tray was in working order and properly inserted. All the little wires seemed to be correctly connected to the little wire connectors. Since I could not find anything wrong, I called in the repairman.

He showed me that the darn thing works best when it is plugged in.

— L. A. P.

☆ ☆ ☆

Now that we are into nonprint as a part of the collection we get questions like "Where are all your audiovisual materials on blimps?" and "Is it possible that you have a record of a whale singing?" — Marianne Gregersen

☆ ☆ ☆

Fourth and fifth graders at our school have the opportunity to apply for a position in our closed-circuit television studio, WUTV. The application asks students to explain why they would be an asset to the WUTV crew. One girl, a fourth grader, said among other things, "I know how to use my diaphragm." Diane Valovich

A note received by Jo Chinn:

Mrs. Chinn,

The filmstrip projector must have been made in Plymouth Colony by Squanto's Optiques, Ltd. (We're talking old!)

Yours in A.V. antiquity,

G. F.

Media Definitions

- *media professional*: Someone with so much education he won't run a movie projector anymore.

- *media specialist*: Librarian who can run a movie projector.

- *IMC*: Library with a movie projector.

- *software*: What hardware becomes after you drop it a few times.

- *VTR*: Very Troublesome Recorder.

— The Medium, 1971

Then there was the time a small child rushed into the library to tell me that there was an emergency in her room, and I was needed RIGHT AWAY! I hurried into the room to find a sobbing mound of 16mm film and a nearly hysterical teacher.

The teacher had instructed her class to sit on the floor of her small room to view a film. The image on the screen was smaller than she wanted, so with the film running, and the lights off, she rolled the projection cart further back. She did not realize that the take-up reel had lodged against the wall causing the film to spill to the floor.

A little boy was sitting on the floor at the back of the class, and since he was well behaved, he didn't say anything as film started to cover him. It was, alas, a long film. By the time I arrived he was virtually covered in film, and extremely upset.

I eventually unwrapped the 16mm film from the angry, crying boy. Naturally, the teacher blamed me and my "stupid projector" for the problem.

A few weeks later the same teacher came into the library, and said in a stern, icy tone, "That projector you gave me does not work. It's running, and everything's moving, but there is no picture. I want you to come and fix it right now! And it is not my fault!!"

Upon entering the room I had to bite my lip to stop from laughing. The screen was in one corner of the small room, in the other corner was the running projector.

She had obviously taken steps to correct the previous situation, and indeed, no film was on the floor or covering her students. What she had done was to move the take-up reel away from the wall by rotating the projector 180°. This also caused the lens to point to the corner opposite the screen. The picture was a two-inch blur in that near corner!

I strolled over to the projector, and with as much aplomb as I could muster, turned it around, focused it, and sauntered toward the door.

As I left I glanced at the boy who had been previously covered in film. He was once again shaking with tears in his eyes, and also biting his lip to keep from laughing out loud.

—L. A. P.

"Just look at that screen—No picture!! The library always gives me projectors that don't work."

Computers

Where a calculator on the ENIAC is equipped with 18,000 vacuum tubes and weighs 30 tons, computers in the future may have only 1,000 vacuum tubes and perhaps only weigh 1½ tons.   —*Popular Mechanics*, 1949

☆ ☆ ☆

The main impact of the computer has been the provision of unlimited jobs for clerks.   —Peter Drucker

☆ ☆ ☆

Computers let you do four times as much work, at four times the quality, in four times as much time.   —Rich Henry

☆ ☆ ☆

Mary Kramer of Follett's Technical Support staff received a call from a troubled librarian whose system had gone down. Mary could hear many young children in the background, eagerly waiting to check out books. The librarian said, "Please tell me what to do! I've got thirty first-graders standing here and a cursing flasher!"
      —"Computers Even Twist Tongues," *Library Automation News*.
      Reprinted with permission of the Follett Software Company.

☆ ☆ ☆

I was working with 30 sixth graders on 15 computers. One of the kids, in his enthusiasm to look up the answer to a question asked by the computer program, tripped over a cord and unplugged all of the machines.
      The class had been working for 40 minutes and *all* of the material was lost. (Sigh!)   —Roberta Margo

☆ ☆ ☆

We use the Electronic Learning Lab in our library media center to participate in Computer Pals Across the World™. Students use the media center's computers to write letters and work on assignments which are sent to another country via an electronic bulletin board.
      Prior to spring break my class sent its first letters to a girls' school in Australia. When we received our replies we discussed words that my students were unfamiliar with, such as budgie (parakeet), boot (trunk of a car), and torch (flashlight).
      It seems that Australian students also have problems with some of our expressions. Meghan, a 15-year-old Australian girl, ended her letter to Alan, a young man in my class, with "P.S. What are you a hunk of?"
                                          —Sue Ardington

The Macintosh computer network in our library became infested with a virus. One teacher came to me and asked, "Who do you think would do such a thing?"

I explained how a disk could become unknowingly infected, but she still thought the virus must have been intentionally introduced. Then inspiration struck. "Well, I guess some people just don't practice 'safe disk.'"

"What!?" she incredulously replied.

"Well, it is okay," I seriously told her, "to use an unprotected disk in your own machine, but you really have to be careful when you stick your disk into a strange computer."

"Nawww ...," she said.

"Yes! And you know those plastic wrappers that come with new disks? You do know that those are disk condoms, don't you?"

"Nawww ...!" again was her rejoinder.

"You bet! You haven't thrown yours away, have you?"

"Well, yes"

"If you are going to stick your disk into unfamiliar computers, you really must take precautions. Disk condoms prevent viruses from being written onto your disk. The nasty little virus programs cannot go through the plastic."

At this point I saw that she was actually starting to believe me. I suddenly was overcome with visions of digging bits of plastic from all of our computers' drives, so I owned up to the truth.

For a small person, she packed quite a wallop.   —L. A. P.

☆ ☆ ☆

The day before I was scheduled to bring my freshman geography class to our library's computer lab, a computer virus had been detected. In the process of cleaning up the problem the library staff distributed a bulletin asking that everyone in the school have their data disks disinfected.

As I was explaining the assignment to my class, a girl raised her hand and said, "I don't think we should go down there; it isn't safe. Didn't you hear that they have a virus down there?"   —Rich Liles

☆ ☆ ☆

The next-door sixth-grade class had just returned from their week-long outdoor education camp when the teacher began using her Apple computer. After being on long enough to warm up, the teacher noticed a foul smell and asked me over to her room to see if I could detect it also. I did, but neither of us could locate the source.

The next day, after the computer had been on all day long, the smell was even stronger, and she again called me over. As we were standing near the computer trying to figure where it was coming from, I heard very tiny squeaking sounds coming directly from the computer. Curious, I set the monitor off to the side and removed the cover to the mother board to discover a nest of mice in the center as the mommy mouse scurried behind the power box. My colleague held her hand over her mouth in disbelief as I remarked to her, "I didn't know you had a mouse-driven computer!"

—Jon M. Higley

I brought my shop class to the library so that my students could design a spread sheet to track individual component costs as well as keep an automatic total of all expenditures. As we entered the lab on our first day one boy, upon seeing his first Macintosh, picked up the mouse, and asked, "Is this what they call a ... turtle?"
— Steve Kostanich

PART 4 THE SCHOOL AND COMMUNITY

Education

Education makes a people easy to lead, but difficult to drive; easy to govern, but impossible to enslave.   — Lord Brougham, 1828

☆ ☆ ☆

It is not of so much consequence what a boy knows when he leaves school, as what he loves. The greater part of what he knows he will speedily forget. What he loves he will feed on. His hunger will prompt his efforts to increase his store. The love of good literature is, from every point of view, the most valuable equipment with which the school can send its boys and girls into the world.   — William DeWitte Hyde, 1909

☆ ☆ ☆

We require so little memorization by the student that the memory, as a practical tool of everyday life, is in danger of falling into disuse.
                    — Arthur E. Bostwick, 1915

☆ ☆ ☆

Many children who might finish high school, drop out because the curriculum will not stand the test of common sense and reality. The academic conception of bright children is based upon their ability to memorize, not to do or to think.   — Sophy H. Powell, 1917

☆ ☆ ☆

The State by constitution is committed to the doctrine of education, committed to schools. It is committed to teaching the truth—ought to be anyway—plenty of people to do the other.   — Clarence Darrow, 1925

☆ ☆ ☆

Education is an admirable thing, but it is well to remember from time to time that nothing that is worth knowing can be taught.   — Oscar Wilde

Soap and education are not as sudden as a massacre, but they are more deadly in the long run.   — Mark Twain

☆ ☆ ☆

If a subject becomes totally obsolete, we make it a required course.   — Peter Drucker

☆ ☆ ☆

Indeed one of the ultimate advantages of an education is simply coming to the end of it.
                    — B. F. Skinner

☆ ☆ ☆

If Rip Van Winkle were to wake up today, he would feel most comfortable in the classrooms of America.   — Bob Hughes

☆ ☆ ☆

Education is a method by which one acquires a higher grade of prejudices.
                    — Laurence J. Peter

☆ ☆ ☆

Let the learner direct his own learning.
                    — John Holt

☆ ☆ ☆

The message out of the state capitals is: We think you [school] superintendents and principals and teachers are a bunch of idiots, so we're going to *tell* you to spend this number of minutes on this subject, and we'll provide a standard set of materials and standardized examination to make sure you follow orders. At a time when the [Reagan] administration in Washington is claiming that our biggest sin has been to stifle initiative by over-regulation, we have entered the greatest era of educational regulation in history.
                    — Albert Shanker

☆ ☆ ☆

States and local jurisdictions have established regulations governing the content of schoolbooks, and they have appointed committees to judge available texts against their guidelines. These committees are not always chosen for their expertise. Membership is often based on politics, geography or role.... [There] is a lack of confidence in the ability of our students to learn from demanding, well-written, good textbooks. Book-adoption committees have relied on "readability formulae" to assign a level of difficulty to given texts. These formulae involve counting the numbers of syllables in words and word of sentences. Writing that is "too complex" may be disqualified for use of a certain grade level. The result? Books with short, choppy sentences, limited vocabulary, homogenized tone and monotonous, unnatural prose style.
                    — William J. Bennett

The fact that Motorola will spend $35 million in the next four years to teach reading skills to its employees, and that by 2001 corporate spending to upgrade workers' skills will reach $160 billion per year are further indicators that educational reform must become a national priority. —Stanley D. Zenor

☆ ☆ ☆

IBM averages $2,200 per year per employee for training. Boeing averages a modest $1,500 per year per employee. School districts average between four to five dollars a year. —Bob Hughes

☆ ☆ ☆

If you think education is expensive—try ignorance.
—Derek Bok

☆ ☆ ☆

I oppose federal aid to education because
no one has been able to prove the need for it.
—Ronald Reagan

☆ ☆ ☆

Schools are now asked to do what people
used to ask God to do. —Jerome Cramer

☆ ☆ ☆

An education isn't how much you have committed to memory, or even how much you know. It's being able to differentiate between what you do know and what you don't. It's knowing where to go to find out what you need to know; and it's knowing how to use the information you get.
—William Feather

☆ ☆ ☆

What facts a student should know is the least important part about a child's education. A student can cram in information, but unless he really understands it, it's easily forgotten. —Mortimer Adler

☆ ☆ ☆

There are some things to be said for rote and memorization and getting the facts and getting the answer right. We Americans, being a pragmatic people, would therefore be well advised to learn what we can from Japanese education—if only because of its manifest success. —William J. Bennett

☆ ☆ ☆

Measuring school success by using test scores is like using body counts to measure the success in Vietnam. —Albert Shanker

☆ ☆ ☆

In schools today there may be a distinction between education and custodial care, but it's wearing thinner every year. —Gerald Raftery, 1964

Our particular hair shirt is called "core curriculum." It is one of those modern educational developments that the ivory-tower desk jockeys are likely to call revolutionary and which the classroom teacher describes merely as revolting.   —Gerald Raftery, 1964

Rules for Elementary School Teachers
1872
(A bulletin of the Piedra Valley Parent-Teachers'
Association, San Mateo, New Mexico)

Each teacher will bring a bucket of water and a scuttle of coal daily.

Men teachers may take one evening a week for courting purposes, or two evenings a week if they go to church regularly.

After 10 hours of school, the teacher should spend the remaining time reading the Bible or other good books.

Women teachers who marry or engage in unseemly conduct will be discharged.

Any teacher who uses liquor in any form, frequents pool halls, taverns or gets shaved in a barbershop gives cause to suspect his character.

The teacher who performs his labors faithfully and without fault for five years will be given a pay increase of 25 cents per week, providing the board of education approves.

Each teacher should lay aside from each pay a goodly sum of his earnings for his declining years, so that he will not become a burden to society.

Administration

A letter received by a school placement officer:

Gentlemen:

Can you furnish us the name and address of a lady who meets the following requirements:

1. She must have 24-30 semester hours credit in library science.

2. And a state certificate covering home economics.

3. She should also be able to teach some few other subjects; though it would not matter so much what those other subjects would be.

4. She must be able to keep pupils quiet and busy — or at least quiet in the library, study hall, or classroom. She should be a good disciplinarian, able and willing to accept responsibility. In addition to the above requirements, it is also expected that she would be willing to do some part in the supervision of playground activities, directed play, hall duty, and be an all-round good teacher.

— *Preparation for School Library Work*, 1933

The following letter was written by a capable young woman recently graduated from an accredited library school, the locality alone being disguised:

I am still as enthusiastic about library work as I ever was and feel more than ever that it is what I want to do, but this year has about made me decide that I was not meant to be a school librarian. The "powers that be" and I do not agree about a "library atmosphere" and I cannot maintain the death-like quiet insisted upon and at the same time do other things — such as catalog, compile bibliographies and all those things I'd hoped to do when at R____. I'm a policeman who scowls menacingly when a child moves to get another book or wants to browse, for I have to answer for any and all noise. I have no chance to put into practice any principles of book selection because all books are sent to my desk and my only task is to accession, classify and catalog them. Even to whisper is so sternly frowned upon that I even hesitate to do reference work or suggest books that I feel would appeal to this and that child — and yet, I'm in one of the best schools in Q____, have a beautifully equipped library and should be satisfied.

— *Preparation for School Library Work*, 1933

The conviction is spreading that there is nothing sacred about local administration, and that the state and eventually the nation should help to build up an educational system in keeping with the dignity and responsibilities of this country. In the business of educating citizens for a democracy, there is no place for outworn political fetishes.　　　—Sophy H. Powell, 1917

☆ ☆ ☆

The more one learns of children, the more is he inclined to think that it may be the makers of school programs who are "backward," "dull," and "stupid," instead of the children.　　　—Sophy H. Powell, 1917

☆ ☆ ☆

School authorities have not come to any definite decision concerning the status of the school librarian.　　　—D. S. Watson, 1933

☆ ☆ ☆

The school administrator has so many jobs these days that if he has an especially competent librarian, he forgets about the library. He can't forget his football team because the community will not let him do so; he can't forget the other services of that nature, but not much pressure usually is put on the school administrator insofar as the school library is concerned.
　　　—John E. Hansen, 1948

☆ ☆ ☆

We have heard many times the statement coming from the administration that the librarian is the person within the four walls of the library. No school librarian can actually serve the school unless she is in all parts of the school. The school must be within the library; the library walls must be within the school.　　　Dora Leavitt, 1948

☆ ☆ ☆

Modern school architects regularly provide for a library room in their plans for a school. Almost as regularly, the school becomes overcrowded and the administration converts the library into a classroom.
　　　—*Teaching the Bright and Gifted*, 1957

☆ ☆ ☆

We recently visited a school where the principal led us confidently down the hall to a dimly lit room about 6' × 12' lined with bookshelves holding multiple copies of tired textbooks. "This," he proudly announced, "is the school library."

Noticing that the books had been classified and cataloged, and knowing that the school had no librarian, we asked who had done the work.

"I hired a retired librarian for the first part," he replied. "Then, I did the rest myself," he said, his voice swelling with pride.

"Oh," we said, trying to sound interested, yet noncommittal. "That must have been a lot of work."

"Naw! Nothing to it," he said. "I just looked for a book on the same subject and gave the new one the next number."　　　—Judith K. Meyers

School librarians continue to struggle against school policies which allow teachers and administrators to use the library as a "Siberia" to which they banish children who are disrupting classes.   — Jim Trelease

"I'm sure you won't mind watching the 'In-House' Suspension class during lunch."

I used to place humorous or thought-provoking quotes each day on a bulletin board in the library. Imagine my surprise when I came in to work one morning and saw the school board had held a meeting in the library the previous night, and sat directly under a quote attributed to Mark Twain:

In the first place God made idiots. This was for practice.

Then He made School Boards.

—L. A. P.

☆ ☆ ☆

A new assistant superintendent, in charge of district school libraries, said upon introduction, "I want you to know right away I don't like libraries, and I hate librarians."   — Mary Sleeman

And then there was the day the production staff was observed rolling around on the floor after reading a request for the following sign:

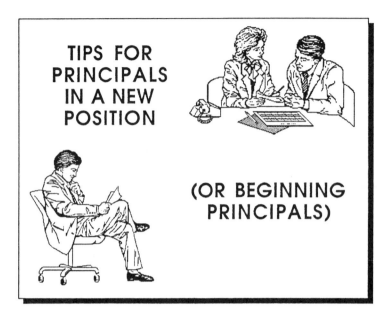

— Judith K. Meyers

Teachers and Staff

The teacher should come to the library and find out for himself what books it contains which may help him ... and his pupils, then he should bring his pupils to the library.   — A. W. Robertson, 1896

☆ ☆ ☆

Apropos of reference work, please look upon me as pleading with you in the name of all librarians of the country, when I say this. Don't draw out all the books of the library on a subject, and then send your class to the library to look up that same subject in those same books. This is the universal crime. When the class comes in we may explain all day that the books are out. The answer is ever the same, "But Miss Smith said we would find the books in the library." I wish this was an unusual thing. But it happens daily. Please, please don't.   — *How the Teacher Can Help the Librarian*, 1907

☆ ☆ ☆

From the library point of view I have learned that she commits the cardinal sin who takes all the references on a given subject and then sends a class to the library to look that subject up!   — Isabella Austin, 1909

After all this I began teaching, with no knowledge of the resources of a library as an aid to either teacher or child, and I felt no *need* for such aid. What is true of me is true of thousands of other teachers.

—Isabella Austin, 1909

☆ ☆ ☆

Someone once asked an old lady how many children she had. The answer was: "Five; two living, two dead and one teaching school."

—Anonymous, 1909

☆ ☆ ☆

The teacher untrained in the use of books and other reading-matter is the weakest link in the school library chain.   —O. S. Rice, 1913

☆ ☆ ☆

[This is] a story told me by an English teacher. A boy had been told to tell the plot of *Tom Sawyer*. "But I can't find a plot," he protested. "You must," was the reply. He returned to his seat and again thumbed the pages. Presently he appeared at the teacher's desk and pointed solemnly to these words, "Any one attempting to find a motive in this story will be prosecuted; anyone attempting to find a moral will be banished; anyone attempting to find a plot will be shot."   —Irene McDonald, 1923

☆ ☆ ☆

Of course, the teacher nowadays has to contend with a multitude of competitors for the student's time and attention.   —Willis H. Kerr, 1925

☆ ☆ ☆

For every person wishing to teach there
are 30 not wishing to be taught. —W. C. Sellar

☆ ☆ ☆

Usually the librarian—actually the library aide—gives you an inventory sheet of all the books you have and you take it, have someone count up how many books you actually have, and then, since you never have the right amount, you invent how many to put under Lost, Missing, or Discarded.

—James Herndon

☆ ☆ ☆

I was told to watch a certain class entering the library with their teacher bringing up the rear. It seems he would often bring his huge class to the library and then duck out for coffee and cigarettes. As the librarian was telling me this the teacher told his class, "I've been called to the office. Don't bother the librarian. If you can't find what you're looking for, go to the big box with the little drawers in it."

At this point the librarian took the teacher out into the hall, and spoke in loud and bold words, "If you EVER AGAIN refer to the card catalog as a 'big box with little drawers' I'll murder you with my own hands!"

—Dar Sisson

You go on and on trying to turn life into lesson plans.
— Richard Peck

"Poor planning on your part does not constitute an emergency on my part."

A teacher at Olympia, Washington, brought her class to the library to do reference work. One girl needed help finding information and the teacher selected a religious reference book. As the teacher was thumbing through the book and showing the girl various sections she turned a page and found a condom. Without skipping a beat the teacher pocketed the condom and continued instructing the student on the book's finer points.　— Sue Pattillo

☆ ☆ ☆

I received a telephone call from a retired teacher when her now-teaching ex-student wished to know the title of a book he had enjoyed while in her class. "It had a devil in it," was her only remembrance.　— Gloria Patton

☆ ☆ ☆

When I was cataloging some filmstrips, I said out aloud, "Let me see where Israel is."

Jerry Thompson, social studies teacher, glanced up from the newspaper and answered, "At the east end of the Mediterranean Sea."　— Ruth Robinson

A boy asked me if he could go to the bathroom.

Without thinking, I replied, "Can't you just stick it out here until the end of the period?"   — Tim Grey

☆ ☆ ☆

AN HONEST CHEATER

Moments after calling out a difficult polysyllabic word during a spelling test in my eighth-grade English class, I observed a student craning his neck to see the test paper of the girl in front of him.

Sarcastically I said, "What are you looking on her paper for? She can't spell that word."

"Neither can I," admitted the boy.   — Daniel Nut Tree

Parents

Juvenile court records show that the weakening of parental control and authority ... is a direct cause of juvenile delinquency.

— Sophy H. Powell, 1917

☆ ☆ ☆

In the average American family, adults spend more time brushing their teeth than talking with their children. That is why tooth decay is down and dropouts are up.   — Attributed to Stanley Pogrow

☆ ☆ ☆

A student borrowed the *B* volume of our *World Book Encyclopedia* over the weekend. The book was never returned despite letters and calls to the parents, who insisted their son must have returned the book because he claimed innocence. This was a particularly touchy situation because one parent happened to be a school board member.

In April the *B* volume reappeared. The boy and his mother sheepishly returned it. During a thorough spring cleaning they found it sandwiched between his mattress and box spring.   — Roz Goodman

☆ ☆ ☆

While weeding the library collection, I asked my aide, Tom, to pull a particularly old, worn book from the shelf and find out when it had been checked out last.

Tom turned to me laughing, and said, "My dad was the last to check out this book in 1945!"

I told Tom to take the book back home to his father and ask whether the book was still interesting in 1980!   — Steve Smith

I am an elementary school librarian and I also run a "Parents and Children Reading Together" program which I incorporate into the school's library program.

The purpose of this program is to encourage parents to spend time reading to their children. I established the reading requirements: The children and their parents or reading partners were required to read together for 15 minutes a day and for a minimum of 20 days out of the designated month. The program lasted for six months of the school year, and monthly reading calendars were sent in to me as special awards and prizes were awarded.

At the end of the last month of the program, a zealous mother very honestly said that the time was running out during the month and that on the very last day of the month for this program, her child fell asleep, but she still "read to him for 15 minutes while he was sleeping" so that they could get credit for the day and the monthly reading.

That's perseverance and dedication! I didn't have the heart to reject the calendar.

— Jean Novis

☆ ☆ ☆

My first professional job was at a tiny, rural school. A few weeks into the school year I heard a child shrieking. I dashed out of the library to see what terrible thing had happened. Along with a group of teachers, I ran into the cafeteria to find a hysterical first-grade boy.

He did not like what was being offered for lunch that day and had ordered the cooks to make him something different. The more people tried to explain how the school lunch system worked, the more he hollered and carried on. Eventually he screamed himself into a stupor and was led to a quiet place to cool off before being sent home.

A bus driver arrived to pick up the child. I had seen her come to the school before in a few other "emergency" situations to pick up children and drive them the many miles to homes dotting the dry-wheat countryside of eastern Washington.

"Whatever do you think could be the matter with this boy?" she asked me.

"Oh, I'm sure he's just spoiled rotten." I replied. "His parents probably give him whatever he wants, and he expects everybody else to do the same. His parents aren't doing him any favors, I can tell you," I authoritatively answered.

As she walked out the door to the small school bus, whimpering child in tow, I turned to see my fellow teachers with tears in their eyes, staggering, and holding their sides.

The school bus driver was the boy's mother.

—L. A. P.

After weekly library sessions with second-grade students, trying to make them aware of the difference between fiction and nonfiction books, I was delighted when one of them proudly brought his parents into the library on "Parents Night" to show off the books in our collection. "Over here are the real books," he accurately explained pointing to the nonfiction collection. Then turning toward the fiction titles he proclaimed, "and here are the fake books!"
— Roz Goodman

Two Letters

Dear Library,

The book *Weird Science* is at a friend's house in Seattle. We have asked her for three weeks to return UPS the book & backpack it was in. Obviously she hasn't. She is coming over *this* weekend & has promised to bring book & pack. Please wait a little longer.

Sincerely,

Good Morning Library,

Joe would like to check-out a book called *Winning*. He was told he couldn't because it was for [young adults].
Joe has *good* reading skills. I think he should be allowed to read it.
He's in sixth grade: Twelve years old — He's definitely a young adult here.

Thank you,

[Joe's mother]

5 KID STUFF

Children

Can adults remember what it was really like being a child? With each telling, the tales of our childhood change. The joyous events become more outrageous, and the tough times more difficult. Parents are required to regale children with tales of the good ol' days when they had to walk uphill in the snow (often without shoes), both to and from school, on a road five miles long. It gave one character.

Here is a collection about students by the older generation, with a few items written by the students themselves, just to keep us honest.

It is noted by all librarians that boys are attracted by books of science; but alas for the girls! The fiction draws them irresistibly.
—*Public Libraries*, 1897

☆ ☆ ☆

Many censuses lately made of the reading of this class of people [girls] show that they take very kindly to books meant for boys, and are in danger of accepting for themselves thereby, and all unconsciously, male ideals, and sometimes even wishing that they had been born boys. This, however, is far better, in my judgement, than the gushy love-story of the modern purveyor.
—G. Stanley Hall, 1905

☆ ☆ ☆

Differences in taste are largely artificial. Girls are brought up according to adult ideas of what they ought to like and do. Early in life, they are urged to be "ladylike" and informed as to the things they must learn to care for. In case a girl rebels, she is called a "tom-boy." One cannot wonder that the strait jacket put on by parents and society has given us a girl problem.
—*The Children's Library: A Dynamic Factor in Education*, 1917

"The good old times" and the admirable children who lived in them
appear better at a distance.   —Sophy H. Powell, 1917

☆ ☆ ☆

Six or seven pupils want "something short" on "England in the time of
Shakespeare." They settle down, two to a book.   —Marion Lovis, 1920

☆ ☆ ☆

John and James were in an altercation over a chair. The silence bell had
rung but there was no silence in their corner. Sam, the clerk in charge, being
fat and good-natured, was slow to interfere. The librarian was on pins and
needles. Finally Sam descended upon the contestants. Grins and giggles
heralded his approach. Followed an investigation, then a "click," and more
laughter. One defender of the chair marched grinning from the room. Sam
returned to the desk and peace immediately enfolded the library. The librarian could not restrain her curiosity. "Sam," she queried, "how did you settle
it?" "Dead easy," said Sam. "We flipped a nickel and John lost."
                                                —Lucile F. Fargo, 1920

☆ ☆ ☆

Our high school has no gangs. What might have been gangs were long
ago metamorphosed into student councils, traffic squads, social-service
departments and rooters' clubs.   —Lucile F. Fargo, 1922

Watch your debate teams ...
they become the reference sharks
of the school.
        —Lucile F. Fargo, 1923

Debate team ... the reference sharks of the library

An eighth grader ran into the media center 30 seconds before he was due in class and gasped, "My reading teacher won't let me into class without a book. What's the thinnest one ya got?"
                                                                — Lee King

☆ ☆ ☆

A young boy wishing to renew his book asked, "Mrs. Holt, I would like this book neutered."
                                                                — Janet Holt

☆ ☆ ☆

Overheard in the library from first-grade boys whose classes had been studying sex education:

"Have you had sex yet?"

"No. I don't even have a girlfriend."

                                                                — Judy Randolph

☆ ☆ ☆

A boy came to the desk asking for the new book by Dolly Parton. "You know, *The Golden Age of Ballooning.*"
                                                                — Eileen Anderson

☆ ☆ ☆

The darling, wide-eyed, kindergarten girl in the very small K-12 school complimented, "You're the best librarian I've ever had!"   — Carol J. Hoyt

A six-foot+ high school boy doing research for a class project asked, "Can you help me find information on the tooth fairy?"
                                        — Margie Thomas

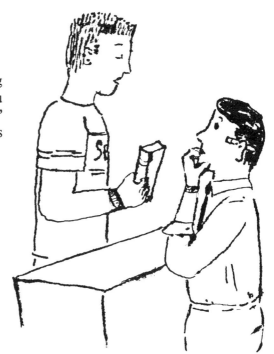

"What da ya got on the tooth fairy?"

The first-grade girl asked if I could help her find the book *Hamburger Bunny*. I was quite certain that she had the title wrong, but rather than embarrass her, I told her that I didn't think that we had that book.

"Oh, yes you do," she said. "I saw it on the shelf last week."

Suddenly it hit me. I located the book *Humbug Rabbit*, by Lorna Balian. "Is this what you want?" I asked.

"Yes," she said. "See, it says 'Hamburger Bunny.'"

—Carol Sue Kruise

☆ ☆ ☆

A student at the Green Hill School, a school for juvenile offenders, came up to the check-out counter with the book *Honor Thy Father*, by Gay Talese. In a know-it-all and indignant manner, he slammed the book on the counter, and to impress his peers standing next to him, asked, "What the hell is this *Honor Thy Father*, by Gay Tails?!"   —Glenda Thompson

☆ ☆ ☆

We placed busts of famous authors strategically about the shelves where their books might be found. One day a student pointed to the bust of Louisa May Alcott and stated, "That's the chick who invented the flag."

—Mary Jane Hill

"WHERE'S THE 'CLIFFS NOTES' FOR THE CIVIL WAR?"

A second grader walking around our reference section asked when he would be allowed to take out those R-rated books. —Susan Hildes

☆ ☆ ☆

From a student book report:

"*Bury My Heart at Wounded Knee* is equal to *Ball Four* in the best book I've ever read category." —Marianne Gregersen

☆ ☆ ☆

Another full day around the library was brightened by the student who came dashing in the door, hurried up to me, and asked, "Have you had a *library* turned in here?" —Judy Carlson

☆ ☆ ☆

Note from a middle school student:

"My mom and I searched practically everywhere in the house for the book. We searched behind dressers, boxes, baskets, under beds, and in bags (backpacks too). We still haven't been able to find it.... I was wondering if you could check for the book again?" —Jo Chinn

☆ ☆ ☆

Scribbled on a study carrel:

"Mr. Johnson and Mr. Parsons are queers."

(The principal and librarian were pleased that the student prefaced both names with "Mr.") —L. A. P.

☆ ☆ ☆

A girl had to write a three-page paper on George Washington. After it was completed she told me that she could not find anything about George Washington in the *F-G* encyclopedia volume, but did find information about Benjamin Franklin, and since the picture of Franklin looked much like one of Washington, she decided to write the paper on Benjamin Franklin, but title it "George Washington." She wanted to know if this might make a difference. —Doris J. Heaton

☆ ☆ ☆

A junior high student asked me, "Do you have any books?" while she was in the middle of the library. —Glenda Merwine

☆ ☆ ☆

I was helping a fourth grader find something in the card catalog. When I asked him if it alphabetically came before or after the guide, he started singing, "A-B-C-D-E-F-G ...," and then, when he didn't hear the letter, he had to sing it again. —Gloria Patton

```
Ruels

Do not kick

No Running

No Throwing books


do not fight


no ripping posters

be certeus to others



Sho in thusiasum

or fake it
```

Posted on library door by unknown
(probably 3rd-grade) author
—Sharon Tyler

When classes came to the library the children took turns being "librarian." They charged the books out and carded return books. One day a small, shy, fourth-grade boy was in the "librarian's chair." A rather large, aggressive girl in his grade kept finding many excuses to be near him at the desk. Sensing his uneasiness, I finally asked him if I could be of help.

He looked up at me and said, "She's been chasing me all recess, trying to catch me and kiss me. I don't go for that stuff, for kissing leads to marriage!"
—Mildred M. Winslow

☆ ☆ ☆

One young man left the library in a huff before we could explain why we couldn't fill his request for a "biography of a horse."   —Mary Jane Hill

☆ ☆ ☆

Early in my career I observed a student carefully going through a card catalog drawer. Occasionally, he would stop and tear out a card. Stunned, I watched him arrange the cards in his hand and go to the stacks to locate the books he apparently needed for an assignment.

I finally raced to him and was surprised to observe that he made no attempt to conceal the cards he had removed from the card catalog. After rephrasing the obvious question several times in my mind to remove the expletives, I asked him what the heck he was doing.

He sincerely replied that he thought you were to remove the cards from the catalog for the materials you needed to find. He believed that we somehow replaced the cards and provided this service!   —Lawrence L. Jaffe

Two sixth-grade boys came to the library after school to check out magazines. One was Protestant and the other Catholic. The Protestant student checked out several magazines because he said that he had to go to church that night and that it is so boring.

The Catholic student replied, "I'll say. I know everything that is going to happen before it happens."

The Protestant student said, "It's not that way at my church. We never know what's going to take place."

The Catholic student agreed, and said, "I know; I went to one of those Prostitute churches once and didn't understand a thing that was going on."

—Alvin G. Rogers

☆ ☆ ☆

A kindergarten class was being read to and one child noticed that someone had drawn in the book with crayon. Another child said, "Oh no, that is just confetti [graffiti]."

—Susan Hildes

As educators we should never assume our students understand what we say—or what we print on signs.

Our high school library regulations required that each student sign (1) name and (2) home room number on the card when checking out material. Never mind the fact home room number was mentioned, repeated, and then stressed carefully to students during library orientation in September. Every time a student started to check out a book, "What room number do I put down?" was asked.

In despair I had a beautiful sign (black on white, 7" × 18") printed that said, "TO CHECK OUT A BOOK, SIGN YOUR NAME AND HOME ROOM NUMBER."

The next time I heard, "What do I put on the card?" I smiled and pointed to the new sign on the circulation desk. The student looked puzzled, hesitated a moment, then signed his name and home room number on the bottom of the sign!

—Luanne Scheurman

A kindergartner who was barely able to see over the check-out counter was printing his name when he looked up with stricken eyes and said, "Oh God ...," as his full bladder took control.

— Gloria Patton

☆ ☆ ☆

I had assembled a small group of first graders around my rocking chair for story time. Naturally, each child wants to get very close. During the middle of my story I felt a little, soft hand first rub my ankle, and then my calf. Rather than disturb the students listening, I decided to wait until the story was finished before stopping the child.

When I completed the story, I looked down at a little boy, and before I could reprimand him, he smiled and said, "Your leg feels just like my mother's."

What could I say?

— Nancy Stanford

☆ ☆ ☆

One June day — six months after Christmas — I was preparing to read *Tar Beach* to a group of kindergartners. I explained that in this story the "tar beach" was the roof of the apartment building in the city. We talked about tar and roofs, and I said that the children of *Tar Beach* play some of the same games that the kindergartners play at a real beach.

Immediately, many hands went up. "I saw a crab at the beach." "I saw a sea gull." I saw a fish." Following up on this line of thought, I asked, "What kind of animals might the children in this story see on their tar beach?"

Amanda's hand shot up. She said, "Reindeer." — Anne Filson

☆ ☆ ☆

A student comment:

"Why should I pay for the book? I didn't even like it!"

— Ann Patterson

☆ ☆ ☆

Lorenzo, a kindergarten student, was looking at a magazine and dropped it on the floor. He said, "Mrs. Roller, will you hand me my magazine?"

"Lorenzo, you should pick it up," I told him.

"Why, are you old?" he questioned.

"Well, I'm getting pretty old."

"You don't look old; you look *new*"!

— Ernestine B. Roller

☆ ☆ ☆

It always bothered me when students were filling out their class schedules that they signed up to be a "Library Ass." Unfortunately, some of them turned out to be just that! — Erma Berkley

An extremely upset high school boy came into the library one night after school and told me that he had just been unjustly suspended for a week. He wanted me to help him find books on the rights of students so he could clear himself of the charges. We found a book that directly spoke to his alleged infractions, and he sat down to read it.

About two minutes later he jumped up, slammed the book down, and shouted to me as he ran out of the library, "That damn book's wrong!"

—L. A. P.

☆ ☆ ☆

Can YOU be scared?

I was bending down to take books from behind the charge-out desk in what I thought was an empty library when Jim, a student in my seventh-grade home room who had some learning disabilities, said, "Boo!" Watching me jump out of my skin, he continued, "Guess I really scared you."

Since this was inappropriate behavior, he and I marched to the principal's office, where I left Jim and returned to the library. In about five minutes the principal opened the door smiling to himself. Jim had explained that seven days previously, during a review of his behavior, I had told him that he "couldn't scare me." While I meant it was inappropriate behavior to scare a teacher, Jim had lurked for an entire week to show me that he could, indeed, scare me.

—Blanche Woolls

☆ ☆ ☆

In a farewell letter:

Dear Librain [*sic*],

Goodbye! I'll miss you.

—Catherine O'Hara

☆ ☆ ☆

A rather short fourth-grade girl asked me if I had a copy of *Treasure Island*. When I asked whether she wanted it in hardback or paperback she replied, "I'd like it in hardback. It makes me look older"! —Volkert Volkersz

☆ ☆ ☆

I was asking a group of seventh graders to tell me the title of the best book they ever read so I could include their choices on a bulletin board. One little "street kid" waved his hand frantically and I called on him.

He said *Charlotte's Web* was just wonderful.

Since E. B. White had recently died, I asked him if he knew that the man who had written *Charlotte's Web* had just died.

He got a stunned look on his face and blurted, "I never knew Rock Hudson wrote that book!"

—Liz Stumpf

☆ ☆ ☆

The first grader who was ready to write his name discovered the borrower's card was full, and said, "Oh, oh. I'm too late." —Gloria Patton

Susan and I had never really been fond of one another throughout her intermediate grades. When she arrived in junior high, I thought of trying to change things, and asked her to join my library club; and she did, which surprised both of us.

Two semesters later, she was putting plastic jackets on books. After putting the jacket on two times upside down, she called to me and said she couldn't get it right side up. My response was "Don't be silly."

"Okay," Susan said, "you do it."

When I did, the book was still upside down because the book had been bound that way. Susan looked at me and said, "Don't be silly!" whereupon we both began laughing.

We've been friends ever since.

—Blanche Woolls

☆ ☆ ☆

A police officer was working with the kindergarten class to help them recognize various traffic and pedestrian signs. As he came to each sign he would ask if anyone could tell the class what the sign meant. Most signs were immediately recognizable to the majority of the students, but when he came to a sign that showed the universal *no* symbol over a picture of a thumb, only Michelle ventured an answer: "No thumb sucking." —Maryann Goree

☆ ☆ ☆

A student asked me for information on euthanasia and I told him to look at the pamphlets in the vertical file. He came back some time later and reported that he had gone right through the *Y* drawer and couldn't find anything. (He was spelling it "youthanasia.") Later, as I told the teachers in the lunchroom about this misspelling, they suggested this definition:

youthanasia: The mercy killing of teenagers who can't spell.

—Linda Brake

☆ ☆ ☆

On the day of President Bush's inaugural address I had a group of kindergarten students in the media center, and after we had checked out books, I suggested that we go into our TV area and watch the new president being sworn into office. If the students would rather look at their books instead of watching, it would be okay.

Most of them watched very intently, and after about 10 minutes one of the little boys raised his hand; since I was eager to hear what he had learned from watching I called on him.

He said, "Ms. Stanford, where is George Washington?"

—Nancy Stanford

☆ ☆ ☆

Recently, during one of my elementary library classes, a second-grade student asked for a "Pee-Pee" Longstocking book. —Helen Fagan

In St. Croix, U.S. Virgin Islands, I was librarian of a K-8 school that was totally without color. The building was grey, and surrounded by brown dirt which the kids kicked into clouds of dust. To make it worse, they had to wear *brown* uniforms. Marina Pukinsikis, the art teacher, agreed with me that whoever chose that color deserved to be required to wear it!

Since the island was poor, there was little money for supplies. Marina made do with whatever scraps she could get and decorated her room, as I did the library, with money from her own pocket. Needless to say there were no colorful bulletin boards in the grey halls.

One day Marina had a great idea. Down the hall from the library were four display cases built into the walls. The glass doors were long gone, but, she said, we could buy some bright colors, paint the insides, and fill the cases with tacked-up kids' art; anything to brighten a beige world.

The next day we started. We'd just finished painting the inside of one case bright orange, when down the hall came a skinny little boy around seven, humming and bopping his way to the office.

We stood back as he cruised on by. He didn't notice us, but he suddenly jerked to a stop, backpedaled to our display case, and said in a tone of wonder,

"Hel-LO Orange!"

Giving the case a friendly wave, he went off smiling from ear to ear.   — Carol Hole

A child came to me and said, "I need a bookworm."

I asked, "Bookworm? Why do you want a bookworm?"

"You know, to keep my place in the book," he replied.

— Susan Hildes

When I was a school librarian at a coastal resort town in Washington state, I used creative dramatics and turned little boys and girls into books to demonstrate a book's proper care and handling. It was a fun lesson which both the students and I loved.

On one particular September weekend I found myself at the rear of the local supermarket picking up some odds and ends. The aisles were jam-packed with tourists enjoying the end of the salmon fishing season.

Two little girls, sisters, ran up and gawked at me. I was dressed in my normally shabby weekend attire.

"Hi there!" I said, recognizing two of my students.

They froze a moment, looked at each other, then ran to the front of the store, giggling and yelling at the top of their lungs, "Mommy!! Mommy!! There's the man who did the funny things to us! There's the man who did the funny things to us!"

The mass of tourists parted, their eyes glaring accusingly at me, as I walked the gauntlet to the front of the store where I found the mother and daughters. I was thankful that she understood my predicament, even if the tourists wondered.

—L. A. P.

☆ ☆ ☆

As spring approaches, the hormones of our middle school students begin to flow. An eighth-grade girl waltzed into the library one sunny morning and matter-of-factly asked if we had any perfume she could use before her boyfriend's bus arrived. She seemed truly surprised when told we did not offer that service.

— Judy Carlson

☆ ☆ ☆

While working on a history project dealing with Albert Einstein, a student asked me one of the classical questions that has defied explanation since 1905. "Mr. Miller, would you please explain $E = MC^2$?"

— Craig Miller

☆ ☆ ☆

A second-grade boy loved to come to the library after school to "help" me in the library. In fact, he considered himself my assistant. One day I heard him direct a student who was returning a book, "Just put in there on the dump truck." Evidently my enunciation of "book truck" hadn't been very clear!

— Mildred M. Winslow

☆ ☆ ☆

I overheard the following conversation between two young men, probably junior high or early high school age, who were in the biography section looking for a book on which to do a report:

"Hey, here's one on Herbert Hoover," said one young man.

"So?" said his friend, "What did he do that is so important?"

"Isn't he the person who invented vacuum cleaners?" asked the first young man.

— Diane C. Skorupski

One of my most delightful students was a bright little boy who has cerebral palsy. He has problems with his speech and has a pronounced limp. He doesn't consider himself to be handicapped, which I learned on a beautiful spring day during the break-dancing craze. Though only a first grader at the time, he came into the library during his lunch hour, went directly to the card catalog, and began thumbing through the cards. When asked if he needed help, he replied, "Mrs. K., do you have any books on bweak dancing?" Even though he couldn't easily walk, he knew all he needed was a good book and he could "bweak dance," too.　　　　— Peggy Kimmet

☆　☆　☆

Second grader Brandon, old beyond his years, was coming to the library every morning to check out a book and to report on the progress of his father who was in the hospital. He said, "Mrs. Roller, I wrote my daddy a letter last night. Do you want to know what I told him?"

Of course, I was interested. He said, "I told him I hoped he was feeling better, and that I loved him." And, he said, "I told him not to worry—that I was taking care of *everything*—except the taxes."　　　　—Ernestine B. Roller

Upon paying a fee for a lost book, a nervous, distressed seventh-grade girl was assured by the librarian that she would be reimbursed if the book was found.

"Oh, not that, too!" she sobbed in reply.

—Sandra Gower

☆ ☆ ☆

A sixth grade boy asked me if "the library had encyclopedias old enough to have anything in them about dinosaurs?" I think he actually expected the encyclopedia to be carved on stone tablets!! —Carol Braden

☆ ☆ ☆

A student asked, "Do you want my phone number here?"
"Why would I want your phone number?" I asked.
The student replied, "This reserve slip asks for a call number."

—Beth Goble

☆ ☆ ☆

I love my K-1 students who want to check out those "dummy" books after I have read and introduced them to *The Stupid Family* books.

—Maureen White

☆ ☆ ☆

A girl returned *Love and Sex in Plain Language* and was asked if she would like to renew it.

She answered, "No, I know all I need to know about it."

—Marianne Gregersen

☆ ☆ ☆

When I was the librarian at a juvenile delinquent detention facility for young men, I used to bring my copies of *National Geographic* to the library. Cathy Dowd, the social studies teacher, would bring her classes to the library and I would let her students have the maps that came with the magazines. These maps became prized possessions (they had so few belongings) which they would display on their walls.

One handsome young man was pouting and visibly upset. Neither Cathy nor I could determine the source of his problem, so we quietly asked him what seemed to be the matter.

He looked at us, then at the boy next to him, and said, "He got a map of the whole world. All I got was sh-tty old Virginia!"

—Barbara Johnstone

"Do you have that book about God?," a young, usually nonreading boy asked me in the school library.

Puzzled, I finally said, "Oh, you mean *Are You There, God? It's Me, Margaret*"? We went to the shelf and it wasn't in. He immediately went over the file of check-out cards and was starting to find out who had the book, but I stopped that. I retrieved it from the girl, who wanted to know why someone else wanted the book. I called the boy back in and handed him the book.

That afternoon there was a group of girls around a table who were obviously working on a project, along with a group of college interns. I went over to see what the commotion was. They did not need any help, but soon they came over and presented me with a petition: "We the girls of the school do not want the boys to read the book *Are You There, God? It's....* It is a very serious matter and they will just make fun of it." The petition was signed by many of the girls including some first graders.

They immediately demanded to know what I was going to do about it. Since the principal was just walking through, I shared the petition with him and he decided that it was important enough to call a meeting of the faculty immediately. Leaving student teachers and aides in charge of the classrooms, we all assembled in the principal's office. The teachers agreed on a course of action which was to be explained to the students at the end of the day.

At the assembly that day, the principal told the students, "Any student can read any book in the library, we would never prevent that; however, if you use anything in the library to hurt somebody, and hurt can be with words as well as actions, we would take action on the fact that you hurt someone, not on the matter that you read something."

That seemed to satisfy the students, but the girls wanted to read a book about boys!
                                                        —Margaret Tassia

The Story of Eddy
by Laila Tedford

I knew his name the first day of school. He was walking around with a grin on his face, the shortest little sixth grader I had ever seen. Clutched in one hand was a sparkling new notebook—empty. In the other was a class schedule telling him to go to the art room which happened to be right next door to the library. So close to his destination his orientation collapsed, and he asked the nearest adult for directions. "Hi, I'm Eddy! Where's art?"

So began a wonderful relationship between a real book lover and a librarian. Eddy came in daily to replenish his supply of library books. He usually had a boxful out at a time and was regularly on the overdue list, but I would never have reduced his library privileges for too many books out.

You see, Eddy lived in a car with his dad and older brother. When it got too cold for that form of shelter, they moved into an abandoned shack and set up house-keeping. Eddy was rarely dressed warmly enough, was usually dirty from head to toe, wore the same clothes day after day, and trailed the odor of wood smoke wherever he went. The books he borrowed and took home to share with his family were, I'm certain, the closest thing to real possessions they had. Eddy had to think of some way to escape from the grim reality of his life.

Eddy was a learner. He always stopped by to mention which books were his favorites, which ones he had really studied, which ones he wished he could keep. He was always enthusiastic, a busy and smiling little guy. And there were lots of things for Eddy to learn about—such as on the day his classmates discovered the 610s in the Dewey classification system.

Several kids were grouped around a few books on human sexuality, growth and development, reproduction, and so on. Eddy was alarmed that materials such as these would be in *his* library and marched over to tell me so. He was undaunted as he pointed out that "Those kids are looking at DIRTY books!" He wanted to know what business I had allowing those books in the library. I explained that the books were very factual and accurate, that students needed to know about their bodies and their development, that I never bought dirty books for our library, just the very best of all informational materials so that our students could always find what they needed to know.

Eddy's eyes widened in astonishment. I think he wanted at first to disbelieve me. Then his expression turned to one of a hungry learner again. "Well then, will it be okay if I check a few of those out?" Yes, Eddy, anything you want, anytime....

The memory of Eddy will not fade. His father pulled him and his brother out of school suddenly the following year. They left with several library books. Oh, well. If I know Eddy, they will be put to good use.

Worst Excuse for an Overdue Library Book

Contest Award Winners from Woodbrook Elementary

"Nessie took my book!"

"I stuck it in the piano and played a note and smashed the book." (first grade)

"I got time-warped into World War I, and my book kind of got smashed by a cannon." (second grade)

"When I was in Washington, D.C., I forgot and left it on the president's desk and he was reading it." (third grade)

"Over spring break I was in New Zealand in our condo when some Libyan terrorists came and burned the house, and the book was nothing but dust." (fourth grade)

"My library books are overdue because the Loch Ness monster ate them! For spring vacation my family went on a European tour. When we stopped in Scotland, we visited Loch Ness. Suddenly a monster popped out of the lake and ate it! That is the truth!" (fifth grade)

—Submitted by Vicki Phillips
and Karen K. Niemeyer

Student Notes

Collected by Marianne Gregersen:

Dear Librarian,

I am returning "Sex" to the library. I hope it does as much for you as it did for me.

Fulfilling yours,

"Me"

A note on the back table said, "The librarian is a Lezbien!"

Collected by Marianne Gregersen
   (*continued*)

A religious tract accompanied this note:

   I didn't plan on returning this book to you, but Jesus Christ has changed my ways. Please forgive me. Happy reading, and God bless you.

A note on the book pocket of *You Would If You Love Me* said,

   Here is *Moby Dick*. I'm so glad I found it! It is truly a beautiful book. I almost kept it.
   Have a great summer,

   Lynnette

P.S. Can I please have my money back?

To our Dear Librarians
Happy 2nd day of
NATIONAL LIBRARY WEEK

Demand:

Get "Publisher's Weekly." *All* mags I want are either "Pub. Weekly" or *gone*.

Love,

If at all possible we would appreciate your investigating into a monthly subscription to "Cosmopolitan" and "Playboy" for our reading pleasure.

Sam

Your service is atrocious. I know that good help is hard to find and that the price of polo pony feed has risen. So get with it.

A friend,

love and kisses

XXOX

☆ ☆ ☆

The next two notes are from Mary Lou Gregory:

To the librarian:

I'm sorry for
the lateness but I
had a temporary mental block.

Mrs. Gregory:

I can't be able to
be in here next year,
on library ass.

Tracy

☆ ☆ ☆

A note received by Diane Valovich:

Dear Mrs. Valovich,

Thank you for helping me on my dinosaur research and how to use a index. What I really like that you taught me is how to draw a dinosaur on a computer.

Love,

Jennifer Lynn

Student Library Assistants Say
the Darndest Things

Compiled by Lawrence L. Jaffe

Those of us who still remember shelving scrolls at Alexandria may recall Art Linkletter's popular TV show, "House Party." Young children were lined up and, despite strict warnings about not revealing secrets of home, last-minute advice about checking flies, and sitting like ladies, were quick to reveal, without inhibition or discretion, such information to millions of viewers.

Over the eons our junior high school library has used an employment form to select students for library assistants. Students are invited to complete an application that includes such things as past library experiences, and reasons for desiring a library position. The honesty that Linkletter discovered apparently persists into adolescence, as was demonstrated by some of our favorites from past years.

Question: Why do you wish to work in the library?

Responses [*sic* throughout]:

To gain experience in bookkeeping.

Because as I help where I can read in piece.

I haven't worked in library, but I shelfed books.

So I can learn to do the job correctly because if I am a librarian, I can get it right.

Just to kill some time and it will give me some experience to help get me a job later.

It gives me something to do instead of reading all the time.

To help out and try to understand the library and things similar with it.

I wish to work in a library because I am fair.

Because I like books and Mr. Jaffe.

I do not know.

Because I have to periods of study hall and 1 of them I would like to get rid of.

I would just like to because I would like it.

Just for fun, and study hall isn't fun.

To stay out of trouble.

To learn more library skills and Mr. Jaffe is a nice person! Ha! Ha!

Because I like books and I would like other people to have the opp. to like them too.

Like Libraries.

To get rid of extra time.

Because I think it would be fun and I would meet people which I think I should since this is my first year hear and I will be here for 2 more.

If I ever need a book it's their in the library and also because it is quiet.

Yes. [a common answer]

Because I like extra-curicural activities and enjoy libraries and have something to do and be a part of.

Because I'd like to be in here and "do" the books. Also because I'd like to hear some more of Dr. Jaffe's wit. [one of my personal favorites]

I wished to work in the library because I like to do homework at home and I am bored in study halls. Also I'm always lost in the library.

Because I think it will help me learn more bout other people, places, and things.

I would liek to work in the library because I love books and it should prove to be very educational.

Because I would like to and I have never before ant It's worth a try.

??

It ofers me a chance to make new friends and to ofer me a mark in the world.

I like to work around people and foul with numbers.

So the library can be open.

To enhance my fellow student, I would like to work in the library.

So I can better understand my library system.

To help out Mr. Jaffe, to earn a letter.

Because our study hall is full. I've always wanted to work in a maximum security prison.

I have some study halls I don't need. I enjoy working there. It's pretty fun, most of the time.

It was fun to help friends find books. I also liked being in charge behind the desk, and carding books was an adventure. [Little did this student know that it is also an adventure for the professional staff!]

Why not make it 3 years in a row at Lionville.

Interested in books, enjoy cataloguing and working with people.
[An amazing response since our students do not customarily do our cataloging!]

... and I like using machines.

I just like to Because I would like it.

To help people in other ways and to know something else about librarys than just a place where alot of books are.

I enjoy the work and the companionship of Mr. (Dr.) Jaffe.

I feel I can be of help here, while in my study hall I would probably just waste time. Besides that I would probably learn more about libraries in general if I worked here.

It is fun to work in the library. I also need to work there for Scholarship Merit Badge for Boy Scouts.

I work like to work in the library because It would be something different and I'm sure to like it. I am a fairly hard worker.

Check out Book. [Apparently this student thought our collection was too small]

Because I Like do those kinds of things, And I enjoy Mr. Jaffe's presents.

It would point me out to good books. I love to read.

For a little responsibility. not alot!

For the pretty blue envelope that appears in my mailbox every two weeks. [Guess who?]

LIBRARY MEDIA
ESSAYS

Telemarketing

I'm mad as hell and I'm not going to take it anymore!

Telemarketing might be a cost-effective method for companies to reach large numbers of library media customers, but that does not make it a legitimate business practice. Telemarketing stinks!

Who are these telemarketers, anyway? Does anybody actually know one, and who would admit it if they did? Can't telemarketers find honest work? Do they have arrest records for working pyramid schemes, or did they previously go door-to-door selling aluminum siding to the elderly?

Could I have once done business with a telemarketer while in a state of delirium? Perhaps I purchased something from one in a former life, and now my name and number has been distributed through a mystical, telekinetic, telemarketing network. Now every metaphysical Tom, Dick, and Harriet with a remaindered book has my number.

So why do they pick on me? If this is someone's idea of a joke, stop it right now! It's not funny. If I offended someone, I'm sorry. Tell me what it was and it will not happen again, I assure you. Just please make them stop calling me!

Why do some sound like my Aunt Mary? I invariably respond to this saleswoman in a tone normally reserved for family members before I realize that dear old Aunt Mary has been dead for a number of years. Once I'm into polite conversation, I just can't seem to shift gears and assume a no-nonsense speech pattern. But they know that, don't they?

Then there are the ones who call and say they were just talking to a well-known librarian in the area. They imply that my colleague, who always happens to be on top of things, spoke of their product in the warmest of terms. When I next see the librarian the telemarketer mentioned, she informs me that she had instructed the bozo to stick his reverse-threaded widget where the sun does not shine, which just so happens to be a very warm place, indeed.

How much can one person stand? Every month or so I get a call from a telemarketer who intimates that we share a long-standing business relationship. Oh, how I hate that. I spend two-thirds of the conversation trying to place the voice, afraid of being rude to a trusted business associate. When the sales pitch is made I realize that I have wasted my time on a charlatan whom I have never met.

Then there is the salesman who hints that I may be the only library media specialist in the nation who is so ignorant as to have never done business with his company. His every word implies that if I buy his junk I will gain acceptance to the "librarian in the know" club. I am sorry to admit it, but a little bit of me wants to belong. What if everybody really does do business with this company, and what if this blabbermouth tells everyone that I don't belong to the club, and what if everyone laughs at me at our next meeting? God, I feel so used and confused.

And how about the gall of the boiler-room hard-sell artists? They must think that we are some kind of stupid. In their world every library media specialist waits expectantly by the telephone, hoping to get a call from a pushy, obnoxious salesman, and joyously encumber the remainder of their budget for unseen products.

These scoundrels will not take no! for an answer. Their game is to wear us down, so we will buy something just to get rid of them. If we tell them that we cannot do business because this year's budget is virtually depleted, they say they will do us this big favor and send the items now, and bill us later! All we have to do is send them a letter with our signature stating that we authorized the transaction. Getting a library media specialist to put his or her own money in jeopardy (remember, the school did not authorize the purchase) must score points with the boiler-room crowd. Perhaps they win a six-pack, or receive some other suitable bonus.

I have always considered myself to be a fairly nice guy. Heck, I am even friendly to door-to-door religion peddlers, but these telemarketers are driving me nuts, I tell you! The trip is short enough nowadays for most library media specialists, and I'm just about around the bend, heading for home.

☆ ☆ ☆

A while back, Roy, a new and conscientious teacher in our building, requested that I introduce his incoming freshman classes to what the library media center had to offer. In talking to Roy I realized I had acquired a "live one"—a rare find off the street.

I wanted to be extra-prepared for a teacher who not only knew what I was supposed to do, but actually came to me first. Frankly, I wanted to strut my stuff. About five minutes before his class was due to arrive, I found myself busy stapling worksheets and reviewing my notes, when I was called to the telephone.

"Hello?"

"May I speak to the librarian? Is she in?"

"I am the librarian." I say. We happen to come in both sexes, idiot.

"Wonderful! How's the weather out your way?"

"It's still raining, and I don't have any time...."

"Great! I know you're a busy man, so let me get down to business. I am Semour Books, and I am your Hi/Lo Hidden Classic representative. As I'm sure you know, our books have been specially treated so that pets will not chew on them! Boy, now isn't that a service an overworked wom—er, ah—librarian like yourself can appreciate?"

"Well, you see, I really don't ..."

"Nips the little beggar's number-one excuse right in the bud, doesn't it? Now I know what you're thinking [not bloody likely], but if you ever get a book that looks like a pet has ravished it, just send it to us and we'll replace it FREE OF CHARGE! No questions asked! How about that!"

"Listen, I simply must ..."

"I can tell you've got things to do. No one has to tell me how overworked, underpaid, and unappreciated you librarians are. I know! So I'll just get to the point. I can make your language arts, special education, English as a second language, and your gifted teachers love you! My company has recently authorized me to send you 1,000 copies of our books for you and your colleagues to preview for two whole weeks with absolutely no cost or obligation! If you should happen to find a few books you might not want, for any reason at all, simply mail them back to us and you will only be charged for those books you decide to keep! Now if you will kindly give me your full name and address, I'll ship these books right out."

Time for my easy out. "I'm sorry, our district requires a purchase order for all ..."

"How silly of me! I've left out the fun part! You may think that each title might cost over $21.95, which just so happens to be the suggested retail price, but listen to this! We supply catalog kits at no extra charge. Now guess the price."

"Gosh, I really couldn't...."

"Wait! That's not all! When you order we will send you your very own 8" × 10" glossy of Melvil Dewey, suitable for framing! Now how much you think you'd pay?"

"Uhhh ..."

"Hold the phone! Dewey's tie clasp is actually a digital clock!! So what would you guess the charge is now?"

"Say, I really ..."

"Would you happen to be married, or have a certain significant other in your life, or just happen to have your eye on someone special?"

"I don't see what this has to do with anything, but ..."

"Say no more. For special, discerning customers like yourself I will also throw in diamond-dust earrings. Diamonds! The gen-u-wine article. The little woman will love you for it. Now if you've got a purchase order number handy ..."

"Listen, even if I wanted to ..."

"District won't let you give out purchase order numbers over the phone, eh? No problem. Every day librarians secure this great limited-time offer using their charge cards."

"What? You actually think that ..."

"Sure. Do it all the time. Standard industry practice. Now if you'll just give me your name as it appears on ..."

"Listen, Buster, why don't you take your books ..."

"Hold your horses! That's not all. I've got oriental carving knives!"

I shout, "Okay, take your books, *and* your oriental carving knives, and #$@*%$%&*!!!"

I slam down the receiver and turn to see a man and about 30 very quiet ninth graders staring at me.

"What do you want?" I hiss.

"Class, this is Mr. Parsons," Roy clears his throat, "and I guess I'll tell you what this facility has to offer."

☆ ☆ ☆

It has been my fortune to meet a rather large number of library media specialists. No group has more concerned and caring individuals. Concern for a good program makes us fight to keep collections viable with shrinking budgets and inadequate support personnel. Caring gets us out on evenings, Saturdays, and even vacations for school activities, professional workshops, and conferences, usually at our own expense. A sincere caring for youth makes us once again experience the horrors of puberty at a level that is almost as good as being there, and requires us to lend a helping hand, sympathetic ear, or a shoulder to cry on when needed. Our concern also gives us the guts to meet and stand up to censors in public forums.

It is these very same qualities that mark us as telemarketing pushovers.

☆ ☆ ☆

It is time for us to do something. Library media specialists are warm, loving people, but even "warm fuzzies" can be pushed too far. It is time to fight. We can do it! I have discovered precious few truths in my life, but I do know one: Library media specialists are not wimps!

Say it out loud, "I am not a wimp!"

Louder: "I AM NOT A WIMP!"

Awwwright!

To arms! We must show these folks that they are playing fast and loose with the wrong people. It is time to purge this cancer from the breast of society. To do so we must hit them where it hurts. We are going to kick them squarely in their bottom lines. We will fight with everything at our disposal. And we will fight to win.

Sacred Rule: Do not buy anything from a telemarketer.

Besides adhering to the sacred rule, be sure to add unique, personal touches of your own. Write letters of complaint. Contact Better Business Bureaus. Simply hang up at the first sign of a sales pitch. Be creative in your battles. This is war. Fighting dirty is permitted and encouraged.

☆ ☆ ☆

The beauty of my favorite telemarketing, terrorist tactic is to do to them what they have done to me: I waste their time. Our telephone system enables me to throw in a particularly naughty little twist. I feign interest to lead them on, and then I put them on hold where they—get this—must endure awful elevator music until they are forced to hang up. I can visualize my craziness flowing into the lines, and rushing straight through to the caller!

When I feel particularly impish, when I am simply itching to reach out and touch someone, I reconnect just long enough to lure them into thinking they might make a sale, only to put them on hold again! Sometimes I catch a worried lilt in their voice which makes me positively giddy. I fantasize that I might be driving the *telemarketers* nuts!

After I have put them on hold for the second time I refuse to answer the telephone for the next hour or so. If a call comes in, I instruct a student to answer it and ascertain whether or not the caller is a salesperson. If it is, the student is instructed to place a hand over his or her eyes, and say, "I just saw the library media specialist a second ago, but I don't see him now. Let me put you on hold and I'll find him."

Telemarketers are correct about one thing. It is great fun to drive people bonkers over the telephone.

—L. A. P.

Things I Didn't Know Going In

More years ago than I care to remember I received my first professional job at a tiny K-12 school as a librarian/language arts instructor. I was immediately and painfully aware that there were a multitude of rules, procedures, and common practices of which I was ignorant. Now that I am getting a wee bit long in the tooth, it might prove helpful for those new to the field for me to note some of the unwritten facts of school life, and share some of the mistakes that I made, because I just didn't know.

I didn't know that the janitor, secretary, and cook are the true power brokers of a school. In the acid test of getting things done the principal comes in, at best, a distant fourth. Never, never, never do anything to upset these people.

☆ ☆ ☆

I didn't know that a good and honest bribe can work wonders. Those burdened with a moral sense might prefer to think of these bribes as tokens of appreciation. Food, drink, and responsibility trade-offs are often the best carrots to dangle. I once got a new bookshelf, newspaper stand, and magazine rack during extremely austere times by using this flow chart:

Buy aide lunch >Discuss with aide (a noted cook) needed improvements to the library >Aide tells janitor with sweet tooth what we would like—hints that there might be a pie in the offing >Janitor makes needed item >Receives pie >Process repeated as needed.

I didn't know that people in education would speak in acronyms, abbreviations, and the latest, most fashionable words. Those aspiring to top administrative positions often massacre sentences the worst. For instance, one might hear from a curriculum director, "The criteria of the ambiguity resides in the actuality that various organizations, i.e., ALA, AASL, AECT, et al., have failed to note benchmark objectives to assure ample amounts of ethnicity be incorporated into selection policies." Nobody, not even the speaker, understands what was said. Most statements like this are made to avoid accountability, and more importantly, to shift blame when the Vigaro hits the air conditioning.

☆ ☆ ☆

I didn't know that every 35th person, on the average, who walks through the library doors would try to sell me something. The exception to this ratio is when the band is wishing to go on tour, then nearly every person tries to sell me something. An interesting observation: You will find that during candy sales, all of the sticky, discarded lollipop sticks and candy wrappers will eventually be found on the library floor. It is one of life's great mysteries.

You will also find some fund-raisers that are not school sponsored. A persuasive young man once convinced me to make a donation to a wonderful sounding youth group. Only after I handed him my spare change did I notice tears of mirth in his eyes, and his friends were struggling to stifle their laughter. A student assistant confirmed my fears when she later told me that I had donated to a kegger.

☆ ☆ ☆

I didn't know that there were school rules that should be strictly enforced, some that can be manipulated, and still others that are generally ignored. Smoking and possession of tobacco can be found in all three areas, depending upon a school's particular situation.

I worked in one school that used to have a unique little ceremony which was repeated at hourly intervals. In an attempt to curtail smoking in the students' restrooms, teachers were required to go in these smoke-filled areas during the breaks between classes. Many teachers disliked this as it cut into their own smoking time. It also required numerous parent-student-teacher-principal meetings as students were invariably caught holding lit cigarettes for their friends. In a rare show of solidarity between students and teachers, this quaint ceremony was established:

Teacher:	Opens restroom door and shouts into billowing clouds of smoke, "Put 'em out!"
Students:	Toss their cigarettes into the toilets.
Cigarettes:	"Psssst! Psssst! Psssst!" as they meet an untimely end.
Teacher:	Strolls into the restroom, observes that nobody is smoking, and leaves.

It might save you time and embarrassment to talk to a seasoned veteran at your school to ascertain which things you are expected to overlook, and which things to strictly enforce.

I didn't know the protocol of breaking up fights. Over the years I have discovered a few universal truths about scholastic pugilism.

A fight is in progress when students are all running in one direction; or when there is a boisterous crowd of students, and this mini-mob totally ignores the teachers.

There will not be a fight if two students threaten to kill and/or maim each other in front of you. They only wish for you to intervene before they do something stupid and get themselves hurt, but after they have saved face.

Obviously it is less difficult to stop younger students from fighting than it is to stop older students. It is much easier to stop a fight after someone has landed a blow. It is also easier to stop a fight between boys than girls. Boys have more fights, but girls usually like to see a fight through to the bloody end.

I once became enraged at a new boy in school when he would not stop fighting. Regardless of what I said to him, he kept throwing punches, even though his adversary was more than willing to throw in the towel. The wrestling coach and I eventually had to pull him off the other boy. As I firmly escorted this new boy to the office, I gave him my lecture on fighting in school, and HOW DARE HE IGNORE ME!! It was only after we were in the office that I learned that he was totally deaf.

☆ ☆ ☆

I didn't know that everybody in the school had a clear vision of the duties of a library media specialist, nor did I realize that no two individuals share the same vision.

We are expected to be a booktalker, A.V. repairer, router of equipment, supply provider, storyteller, disciplinarian, provider of every classic ever written, computer expert, babysitter for the critically gifted, film reviewer, cataloger, study hall monitor, videotape wizard; the list goes on forever. There is only one item on which everybody is in agreement, you must be available whenever you are needed.

Since schools currently attempt to do so much more than provide the Three R's, library media specialists are expected to provide virtually everything, for everyone, and to do anything.

☆ ☆ ☆

I didn't know how many coaching and advising positions are ideally suited for the library media specialist. We library media specialists are perfect for these positions because (1) we work in schools and (2) we are alive.

The chief difference between coaching and advising is that coaching is paid at a rate somewhere near 50¢ per hour; advising is done for something other than monetary reward.

I didn't know how many activities needed faculty chaperones. Chaperones are required for rooters' buses, carnivals, trips, and especially the bread and butter of the ASB (Associated Student Body), dances.

To be a chaperone you must attend a function after school or on weekends, and assume the added responsibility (with no remuneration) of making sure everybody behaves in a socially acceptable manner. Chaperones are also responsible to make sure that the "clean-up committee" puts everything back in order. Therefore, since clean-up committees seldom materialize, the chaperone and one or two students will stay after to clean up, and it will be the chaperone who will endure the wrath of teachers and principals when a table is missing from room 22.

I have never heard of a class being offered in the art of chaperoning, yet every school employee is expected to possess this masochistic ability.

One of my more memorable chaperoning episodes consisted of taking all of our school's sixth graders up into the mountains for a week-long environmental education workshop. I spent my days hiking, teaching, and playing games with the kids. My nights were spent keeping the boys from partaking in various adventures, such as sneaking into the girls' dorms. I had no idea how long I could go without sleep.

☆ ☆ ☆

I didn't know how many guilt trips would be laid on by principals and students, usually in an attempt to coerce someone into becoming a chaperone. Although I cannot prove it, I know that prospective school administrators are required to take classes in "guiltmanship" which are taught at JCMS (Jewish-Catholic Mothers' School).

I was extremely fortunate to be brought up by a mother who graduated with a black belt from JCMS. Now that I am older I can look back and thank her, just as she said I would.

So when a principal comes to me and says, with quavering voice, "I've come to you because I am sure you won't let me down. If I can't count on you, who can I count on? You do realize, don't you, that there is a dance this Friday night? The proceeds from it will go to help crippled, battered children of chronically insane, alcoholic parents with halitosis. I am asking you, begging you, to please help chaperone, to keep our kids off drugs, alcohol, and 'the street,' as only you can."

I look dejected and say, "I know I'll regret this when you're dead, but my wife's sister's husband is sick, my dog has ticks, and I really must wash my hair because of problem dandruff, which may be linked to the AIDS virus, and we wouldn't want to spread that around, would we?"

☆ ☆ ☆

I didn't know that principals actually wanted different bulletin boards constructed every few weeks. I can only remember one from my childhood, and that was because my name kept appearing on the bottom rungs of its achievement ladders.

Additionally, I didn't know that a dry-mount press was a multifaceted appliance which can iron the pleats in cheerleading skirts and heat food.

I didn't know that book budgets would be so puny.

I didn't know that my favorite books would likely be stolen.

I didn't know that the teachers would want to show every film and videotape simultaneously.

I didn't know what to do when a child starts to vomit.

I didn't know that library media specialists were expected to take bus duty.

I didn't know there could be so many creative excuses for lost or overdue books.

I didn't know how much homework was required to give a good booktalk.

I didn't know that this year's projector would not accept last year's lamp.

I didn't know that no two VCRs would record in the same way, and that their counters were all calibrated differently.

☆ ☆ ☆

And I certainly didn't know that I could make up so many stories to hide the vast areas of my ignorance. I wonder if principals and teachers ever dream up stories?

−L. A. P.

Hidden Job Costs

Inequities are so commonplace that we fail to notice them. Whether the cause is survival instinct or preoccupation with normal day-to-day activities, we do not spend a great deal of time contemplating fairness and equality.

Reflect for a moment on:

- The number of women who have held the top two governmental positions in the United States.

- How many NFL head coaches who happen to be black.

- School administrators who actually teach a class now and then.

Most people feel powerless to battle problems of such a global nature. Perhaps if we could learn to deal adequately with the smaller inequities we would be better prepared to tilt larger windmills.

For instance, have you ever added up the tithes we annually make just to keep our jobs? I am not talking about workshops, college transcripts, gas to and from work, or the obligatory uniform of dress shirts, ties, slacks, dresses, skirts, blouses, or sweaters. What I am talking about are the students who come to you demanding that you purchase this or that to support a certain activity. Sometimes parents, administrators, and even fellow teachers get into the act.

Oh, they are sly, aren't they? They figure out that you probably got into the school biz because you genuinely cared about kids. So they sneak up and place a tourniquet around your guilt jugular and start to squeeze. They will say something like, "Please sponsor me in the Special Olympics Dance Marathon." (Squeeze.) "You will buy a candy bar so we can have a baseball team this year, won't you?" (Squeeze!) The band is planning a trip to Washington, D.C...." (Squeeze! Squeeze!)

We all know the scenario. Every word is calculated to make you throw open your wallet and show that you *care*. The more you spend—the more you care. Woe unto the churlish faculty members who do not give, regardless of any reason; because not giving proves that they just *don't care*.

And we all know what happens to teachers who don't care. The community forms a vigilante committee and goes after them! They put the screws to principals, who then have to prove to the vigilantes that they themselves care, by doing something to staff members who *don't care*.

Principals must also join community organizations in an effort to keep their own jobs, thus proving to superintendents and school board members that they *really care*. These organizations, in turn, force their members to sell things. Roses seem to be the product of choice for a number of service groups. Staff members under vigilante pressure who wish to prove that they actually do *care* need to buy these roses from their administrators. (Remember: The more you buy, the more you *care*.) Roses, by the way, are always sold just prior to the teachers' yearly evaluations.

Teachers, especially library media specialists because of flexible schedules, are additionally asked to make "in-kind" contributions. These contributions carry no direct financial burden, but require one to leave home for an evening, weekend, or sometimes even days on end to supervise various activities. We are asked to make in-kind contributions for open houses, fairs, field trips, rooter buses, sporting events, environmental education retreats, wellness workshops, and school dances.

Spouses and significant others seldom immediately understand the need for in-kind contributions. They probably come from a universe that embraces a concept foreign to education: Time is money. In all likelihood they once viewed school employees as working a seven-hour day, having evenings, weekends, and summers off, while relaxing on vacations liberally sprinkled throughout the year. It is quite a shock to learn that there is a cover charge to Paradise.

In a rare fit of administrative intelligence one assistant principal kept a year-long monetary account of what it would cost to buy something from everyone. His findings: If a person bought the single cheapest item from everyone who accosted her or him, the charges would run in the neighborhood of $250. If, however, the person decided to go whole hog and buy a freezerful of frozen pizzas that the band was pushing, and the large, tacky calendars, mugs, boxes of candy, and stuffed animals, the cost would be well over $1,500!

The goal of every school employee, unless, of course, he or she has a child in the band, is to establish an aura of *caring* with as few dollars as possible. But how does one do that? Is it better to purchase a few expensive, unnecessary items from two or three groups, or a little schlock from everybody? And is there a tactful way to turn down these telemarketers-in-training?

For the answers to these questions, and other problems—such as creative uses for a freezerful of awful pizza—send $3.95 (plus $1.00 for shipping and handling) to the author in care of this publisher.*

---

*Just kidding.

For merely $3.95 you will get the latest edition of *Intelligent School Junk Buying: The Biggest Bang for the Buck!* Not only will you learn ways to save hundreds (perhaps thousands) of dollars, but also the proceeds from each and every sale will be used to send the author to an important professional seminar in Australia! You will receive timely and needed advice, plus you will show that you *care* by furthering the educational opportunities of a colleague.

Don't hesitate. Order now! Acquire job security! Be highly regarded by fellow students and administrators! Prove to yourself what a wonderful, kind, and *caring* person you truly are. Do it today!

—L. A. P.

The Locker Check

The military has K.P.; schools have locker checks.

Library media specialists always pull the dirty duty.

Why do people think that scavenging through sweaty socks, jocks, and abandoned lunches in search of the elusive library book is our idea of a wild and crazy time? Since we work with books, I suppose, we are expected to eagerly jump at the chance to reclaim lost, stolen, and overdue books. Checking lockers certainly sends tingles up my spine.

What innocently starts out as a simple search for library books soon escalates into a full-scale shakedown. Notices are published in the bulletin telling students to take the locks off their lockers on a certain day. Rumor has it that by making this public statement the lockers once again become school property, and staff can search them to their hearts' content. After this statement has been run in the bulletin for a certain number of days, the fun begins.

After school on the designated day the library staff, under the supervision of an administrator, hits the halls with book carts in tow. The search is under way!

Teachers are always surprised to see a locker check, since they, like students, seldom read or listen to the daily bulletin. Many are eager to get into the act. At this point the administrator sees the potential for conflict and vanishes, presumedly to form a committee to deal with the problem.

Ms. Touch E. Feeley is first to see you and voice her opinion as she is always out in the halls relating to kids after school. Ms. Feeley wants to make sure you gather books from all of her classes. After all, how can she be expected to teach her overloaded classes without materials? Besides, keeping records of who has what books and keeping students accountable is not her job. She was hired as a teacher, not a bookkeeper.

She also suggests, then later demands, that you find and recover every book from her entire department or grade level. Other teachers need help too, you know.

Mr. Stern R. Stuff thinks the locker check is a grand idea and volunteers to help. With careless abandon he takes every library book, even books that are not yet due. For once in his life Mr. Stuff heeds the words of his arch-nemesis, Ms. Feeley, and takes every book from both his and her departments. Naturally, neither of them are around when the other teachers come screaming to you that *you* have absconded with their students' texts.

Some schools are blessed with a staff member who should go by the name of Loon E. Toons. Ms. Toons (Toons can be of either sex) has supplies in her room that keep vanishing. She sees the locker check as a chance to reclaim lost property. So off she goes collecting scissors, staplers, tape, T-squares, compasses, and rulers. The spirit can move her to such heights that she has been known to collect hundreds of pens and pencils because she knows students have stolen at least that number from her over the years. The locker check is her way of setting the record straight.

Library media specialists should never question Ms. Toons during her collecting frenzy. Just get out of her way. Being stapled to a T-square is not a fun way to go, unless, of course, you seek library media martyrdom.

The sad truth is that locker checks are going to happen, and library media personnel will be involved in them. The universally held opinion of library media professionals the world over is that *locker checks suck.*

As a survival methodology it is sometimes helpful to don the cloak of the inquisitive scientific researcher while doing your dirty duty. The trained observer can find hundreds of topics for contemplation.

- Fashion Trends and Attitudes: Why do students leave clothes that most staff cannot afford unattended in lockers?

- Social and Legal Awareness: How many times, and by which types of students, will you be asked the following questions: "Are you gonna cut the locks off that were not removed?" and "Hey, dude! What you gonna do if you find drugs?"

- Changing Sexual Mores: It used to be that posters of partially clothed and nude women were found in boys' lockers. Then pictures of partially clothed or nude men were found in the girls' lockers. Today it seems to be a 50/50 split. (You will also find pictures from your missing *Sports Illustrated* bathing-suit edition.)

- Culture: Locker decorations will show who and what is currently hot.

- Entomological Science: What insects thrive on moldy peanut butter and jelly sandwiches?

Locker checkers should develop a mantra to chant while sorting through the flotsam and jetsam of the locker bays. While mantras are helpful when dealing with difficult teachers and administrators, they become indispensable while checking lockers. If you really get into your mantra you may not be overcome with nausea when opening the locker that has been secretly used as a trash bin for the better part of a year.

Mantras are, and should be, private affairs, but you may overhear busy locker checkers mumbling their mantras in particularly difficult situations. For instance, my dear friend and assistant helps me with my locker checking because, in all honestly, I am not so stupid as to do it all by myself. Simply put, I make her do it. Anyone with half an ear will recognize her mantra as, "They don't pay me enough to do this stuff." (The astute reader will recognize that *stuff*, while the operative word, is not the actual word.) She often punctuates her mantra recitations with certain gestures and salutes, presumably remnants of her Bohemian heritage.

For those of us burdened with a chronic sense of reality, who cannot chant mantras, mind travel, role play, or who are otherwise preoccupied with the "big picture," I offer this psychic salve. Locker checks, helping at open houses, hosting the PTA, and even (shudder) chaperoning dances are the stuff that slaps the magical grease on the path to the library media center. Things like increased book budgets, emerging technology, and even professional respect will often slip your way if you are viewed as a willing accomplice to these nefarious activities.

Don't ask me why. No time to think. We're off to Freshman Hall, book carts in tow, to find missing library books, contemplate the nature of the universe, and see if anyone is still interested in Michael Jackson.

Sometimes, however, I think they don't pay me enough to do this stuff.

–L. A. P.

Evaluations

I was going through my files the other night and came upon the papers that formally document my professional worth. These were my evaluations from a number of districts, dutifully completed by an even larger number of administrators. For an evening of home entertainment, I heartily endorse reading your evaluations.

After studying these papers at length, about the time it took to do irreparable damage to a bottle of white zinfandel, I came to the conclusion that it is impossible to develop a boiler-plate evaluative tool for the library media specialist.

No two library media specialists have the same job responsibilities, and 90 percent of the evaluators do not have a clue as to what the role of a library media specialist should be. Of the remaining 10 percent, how many would recognize a "selection tool" if they were whacked alongside the head with *School Library Journal*? I have generally been blessed with wonderful principals, yet not one of them possessed the foggiest notion whether or not I could correctly catalog a book or file a card. For that I am thankful.

Schools that encompass identical grades and subjects in the same district are even quite dissimilar. Teaching staffs are made up of unique individuals who implement the goals and objectives of their buildings in divergent ways. The library media specialist's job is to support the needs of the building's curriculum, teachers, and students.

Evaluative forms are a different matter entirely. Most are nauseatingly similar. I vividly remember one evaluation a number of years back. It was not my first job in the field, but it was my first evaluation at this particular school. I entered the principal's office with some apprehension and saw him staring out the window. He looked up at me, and then started rearranging the papers on his desk. At the time I did not realize that he was doing what he did best. After clearing his throat a few times, he handed me my evaluation with directions to sign it on the dotted line.

I started reading the form and found it to be the standard teacher's evaluative checklist used by that district. It had four columns, labeled unsatisfactory, needs improvement, adequate, and outstanding. Not only did little of the criteria pertain to my job, almost all of the checks were in the *adequate* column, with a few *needs improvements* and *outstandings* randomly tossed about. I was outstanding at discipline, and needed improvement at recess duty.

Now that confused me. I kept the library open during recess, which precluded my being outside with the children. Furthermore, as this was my rookie year at this particular school, a few students took great pleasure participating in the ancient and hallowed ritual of teacher baiting. The kids weren't throwing books at one another or shouting obscenities, but I suffered through what I considered to be more than my share of pranks, whistling, and obnoxious noises. I certainly did not consider myself worthy of being formally evaluated as an outstanding disciplinarian.

But what really got my goat was that the evaluation pegged me as being *adequate*. I hate adequate! I'll accept any of the others, if need be. The Seattle Mariners are an *adequate* major league baseball team; nobody follows the Mariners! *Adequate* is a meal at a buffet restaurant. Buses are an *adequate* means of transportation. *Adequate* is apathy's kissing cousin.

Tell me I screwed up and I will try to do better, pat me on the back and I'll strive for excellence, but don't tell me that I'm adequate!

I decided to question some of his observations. He appreciated my discipline as evidenced by the fact that I had sent nobody to the office. Upon further questioning, he hunched his shoulders and informed me that since it was my first year, this was about as good an evaluation as I could expect. When asked about specific items, like my lack of expertise at recess duty, he informed me that the superintendent demanded that he evaluate everyone completely. That meant every item had to be checked!

He strongly suggested that I sign the darned thing if I knew what was good for me. Knowing what was good for me and because he really didn't use the word *darned*, I signed it, and headed for the faculty room with a full head of steam. It was after school; the regular bridge game was in progress. Two veteran teachers were sitting in on the game and inquired about my obvious state of apoplexy.

I showed them my evaluation and they broke up laughing. They had also been evaluated that day, and showed me their evaluations. All three evaluations looked remarkably similar.

It was at that moment I quit working to please evaluators and started working to please myself. I already had informally constructed my own standards, and they were certainly more meaningful than the ones used to formally evaluate me.

Don't get me wrong: I think the concept of having everyone honestly evaluated by competent evaluators is valid—and I mean everyone, including the superintendent and other administrators. My concerns have more to do with the fact that most of our evaluators do not have sufficient knowledge to do a competent job of evaluating library media specialists. Many don't know L.C. from Dewey, wonder why we don't put all of the pretty little red books together on the shelves, and believe MARC records are scratches on LP albums. The thought of a "merit pay" system should make every library media specialist shudder.

Just because a person is an administrator does not necessarily mean that he or she is a stupid, uncaring jerk. Believe it or not, I have empathy for most of the people who have to evaluate us. It's a tough job, and they more than likely have matters that they consider more pressing than learning the complete nitty-gritty of running the library media center. Just be sure they recognize that you work with staff and students with evangelic zeal, and the formal evaluations will take care of themselves.

But just for once, wouldn't it be great fun to evaluate them, and learn our evaluators' levels of library media expertise?

Library Media Evaluation for the Administrator
(Modify to meet your needs)

1. When was the last time you read a book for pleasure?

2. When was the last time you visited the library media center?

3. Which of the following do you have in the library media center?

    ____ 16mm projector   ____ overhead projector   ____ typewriter

    ____ record player   ____ audio cassette player   ____ word processor

    ____ VCR   ____ slide projector   ____ computer

    ____ camcorder   ____ microfiche projector   ____ opaque projectors

    ____ security system   ____ circulation system   ____ telephone

    Which of the above can you operate?

4. On a scale of 1 to 10, where 10 is highest, evaluate the importance of

    _____ library media centers   _____ extracurricular activities

5. a. How many professional conferences do you attend each year? _____

    b. Do you support library media staff who wish to attend theirs? _____

6. How would you likely handle a situation where an irate parent demands that you pull a certain book from the library?

7. What is the cost of the average library book?

8. How many books should be in your library, and how many do you currently have?

9. Compare and contrast the typical duties of the library media specialist with those of an educational assistant who works in the library media center.

10. Describe the perfect library media center.

—L. A. P.

Library Media Stereotypes

Are you more than a little tired of people coming up to you and asking why your hair isn't in a bun? Do you ever experience violent fantasies when someone comes into the library, index finger pressed to lips, and loudly hisses that old knee-slapper, "Shhhhh!" And anyone who works in the library simply must be a woman.

It is high time for school nurses (everyone knows they are not "really truly" nurses), kindergarten teachers (they talk to everyone as though they are speaking to five-year-olds), and, of course, school librarians, to generate a few stereotypes of our own.

"Shhhhh!"

Tunnel visionary: The school community exists as a support system for their classes or activities.

Disciplinarian: The true disciplinarian must have at least 15 years teaching experience. (Experience is waived in the case of former drill sergeants.) They teach while holding pointers and yardsticks. Secondary-level disciplinarians have either mastered their subjects or can fake it. Elementary-level disciplinarians remember, with a misty eye, the good old days of giving hacks. Favorite quote: "Kids don't learn like they used to, and they never did!"

Mr. and Ms. Popcorn: These teachers show films four days per week. On the fifth day they give a test. Students refer to their room as the Roxy.

I'd teach even if they didn't pay me: These teachers genuinely like kids. They also have working spouses. A paradox exists in that they brainstorm ways to get more money, and frequently tutor on the side.

Don't I look mahvalous?: This is usually a jock or jockette who believes that his or her body is a temple which everyone is welcome to worship. They frequently have problems relating to students of the same sex. "Don't I look mahvalous" clothing is recognizable by having certain fashionable logos and words prominently displayed on bosom and/or buttock. Some years the *trés chic* female of the species may sport a golden fingernail; other years, all of her fingernails are of a multicolored hue and design. Males waffle between very narrow and very wide ties. Both sexes drive cars that they can't afford. What three beautiful words are these people deprived the joy of hearing?: "Attention K-Mart shoppers!"

Traffic safety instructor: A male coach takes this job because the administration has nowhere else to put him. If he survives a few years, a metamorphosis takes place. The brash young firebrand acquires a Zen-like countenance. He is at peace with himself. He gains perspective, becomes philosophical, and his I.Q. jumps 30 points. His teams may even start to win! Facing death on a daily basis at the hands of 15-year-olds must be an experience akin to surviving The Black Hole of Calcutta.

Weekend wonder: He greets you at the door on Monday morning and requests, nay, demands that you give him everything the library has on World War II for his first-period class. Weekend wonders will assign every student in a sixth-grade class a report on scorpions. At the secondary level he will assign, to three separate classes, research papers on Islam. He often complains to the principal that the library does not meet his needs.

Hoarder: Behind padlocked closets the hoarders keep their scrounged and treasured stash. They may have cornered the school's chalk market, and dispense broken pieces for small favors. Hoarders may smugly believe that when the ink well once again comes into fashion, they will become the school power brokers. Upon retirement there is a sacred gift of lock combinations to a friend.

Never go homer: Never go homers can be found at school any time of the day or night, as well as on weekends, holidays, and summer vacation. Heaven only knows what they do there all those hours. They are not *that* prepared.

Aspiring administrator: An aspiring administrator is not satisfied with being a teacher. Success requires taking those education classes which were once skillfully avoided, then completing something called an "internship" at his or her school. The internship consists of doing all the things that the supervising principal is loathe to do, with a minimum of sniveling and whining, and at no extra pay.

Library/cigarette break (a.k.a. *dead butt break*): The main reason these persons bring their classes to the library is to leave their charges in good hands—while the teachers go off to smoke.

Misunderstood liberal: The very first week with students was spent trying to *relate*. She (or he) then spends the rest of her career trying to be *understood*. (He always has facial hair and never wears a tie.) She experiments with the latest learning styles, and never uses the same style twice, unless she has been really bummed out lately. She likes supportive people. She sees teaching as a cause, but students usually learn regardless of tactics used. She goes with the flow and is unorderly. Can you dig it?

Subtle conservative: Photographs of Ronald Reagan, J. Edgar Hoover, and John Wayne can be seen tastefully displayed alongside the flag in his (or her) room. Pithy comments from William F. Buckley and Phyllis Schlafly appear on the board from time to time. Class is started with the "Pledge of Allegiance," and students quietly remain in their seats until it is time to go. He is always clean shaven and dressed in a suit or sports coat. (She often dresses in earth-tone skirts.) His lesson plans consist of lectures, liberally sprinkled with rightist comments; readings from texts, which have questions at the end of the chapter for students to answer; and numerous quizzes and tests, administered every Friday. He sees teaching as a cause, but students usually learn regardless of tactics used. This person is rigid and orderly.

Teacher/administrator in search of a baby-sitter: These folks *know* you have a cushy job. They are envious, and at times even compliment your wisdom in choice of vocation. A typical comment: "I'm going to speak to the Rotary in five minutes and have told the afternoon P.E. classes to report to the library." States need to put a bounty on them.

"Sneak-thief" borrower: Are you missing cassette recorders, VCRs, video and audio cassette tapes, TVs, equipment carts, dictionaries, record players, patch cords, adapters, computers, printers, extension cords, 16mm projectors, slide projectors, date-due stamps, ink pads, and anything else not nailed down? And there is no trace of a clue where these items might be? Before calling the police, check the sneak's room. There is a 99 percent chance the missing items will be found there. There is a 100 percent chance that the sneak will think you are overreacting when discussing the problem. On second thought, call the police.

Freddy the fibber: He just has to preview educational material for class at home. Coincidentally, the VCR is returned with bits of popcorn and smeared with birthday-cake frosting.

Extra-credit giver: This staff member brings a class to the library on Mondays, Fridays, and daily for two entire weeks prior to the end of grading periods. The rationale is that the students may do extra work to bolster sagging grades. The teacher either reads, vanishes, or sleeps. Most of the kids talk, play, or skip class, but a few copy sections out of the *World Book* for extra credit.

Polly the procrastinator: Polly orders numerous films and videotapes. She shows them all on the day they are to be returned.

Dr. Ditto: Assignments in his class are ditted. Upon entering class the student greets the teacher, who is usually reading the local newspaper, takes a dittoed worksheet from the desk, proceeds to his or her seat, and fills in the blanks.

Anointed: The anointed has found the answer! Be it religion, ecology, abortion, or what have you, these persons set about enlisting converts and making hidden agendas. At first they put up posters and hold meetings which all students are encouraged to attend. After feeling the sharp tongue of their uninitiated peers, they covertly enlist recruits, and the meetings go underground. The only person more annoying than the anointed is the newly anointed.

Caffeine crazy: He drinks so much coffee that by the end of the day the students watch *him* bounce off the walls.

A.V. kiss of death: This person (frequently a woman, but always an outstanding teacher) can break a sturdy piece of equipment just by plugging it in. In some instances she may be the demigoddess of a student cult as a result of rumors in which her overhead projector experienced a "meltdown" while she was lecturing about Three Mile Island.

Ain't it awful: This final category is for the Rodney Dangerfields of education. Everyone can be one.

"Ain't it awful that

- parents are so unresponsive!"
- beer truck drivers make more money than we do!"
- my administrator is such a jerk!"
- I've got recess duty!"
- I always get the discipline problems!"
- nobody understands my unique problems!"
- I've pulled lunch duty again!"
- I always get the shaft!"

—L. A. P.

Whatever Happened to ...

Taking a book inventory is like going on a trip down memory lane. It seems like only yesterday I was helping kids find books on pollution. Now our ecological books do little more than participate in their own biodegrading process.

Our collections work as a sociological barometer with the circulation records measuring the changes. Today's forecast predicts highs in AIDS, lows in Nuclear Energy, with a storm front of Steroids in Sports moving up the coast. Inland will see storms of Anorexia, periods of Bulimia, and a slight chance of Lyme Disease. The entire country can continue to expect scattered instances of Sex, Drugs, and Rock and Roll.

Have you ever noticed that when a topic heats up people start referring to it by its initials? Sometimes the initials grow up to be acronyms. Maybe some topics would not get so hot if folks refrained from tagging them with cute and catchy little names. Is this because acronyms, like nicknames, are somewhat jazzy, and using them shows the world that one is in-the-know? Or could it be that we are, after all, like children who are more comfortable talking about some things by using made up names and initials? "Teacher! Teacher! Johnny said the *S* word!"

Over the years school libraries have acquired materials on AIDS, TM, NATO, PMS, UFOs, OPEC, VD, DMSO, STP, RNA, DNA, the KKK, and the ROTC.

Today's hot topic can be all but forgotten tomorrow. Before everyone became terrified of AIDS, about half of us were concerned over toxic shock syndrome. We do not hear much about toxic shock syndrome anymore. Perhaps if we had called it TS....

Thankfully, a number of subjects endure. Every year students will want something on Capital Punishment, Gun Control, Animals, Cars, Countries, and the aforementioned Sex, Drugs, and Rock and Roll.

In my rookie season, well over a decade-and-a-hunk ago, in the era of Earth shoes, gas lines, and longer hair, we concentrated more on social issues and our inner selves. Searching for truth was more important then. If the truth got too "heavy," we turned on the tube and laughed at "Laugh-In," or Archie and his son-in-law the "Meatball," as they went at it. Those days a person could also find a copy of "Desiderata" wherever folks gathered, be it living rooms, faculty rooms, or restrooms. We were supposed to "go placidly," you see.

What far-out books we bought! Small presses must have done a booming business. We searched for books on Transcendental Meditation, Homesteading, Overpopulation, Female and Racial Equality, Global Awareness, Nuclear Weapons, Peace, and Zen.

Then we had geared down our speed limits to 55 MPH, and spruced up for our Bicentennial. A warning was issued and we all were supposed to rush out and get vaccinated for swine flu. The pigs (real pigs, not cops) had the last laugh on that one. Eventually an interest in government, public safety, and consumerism developed.

The books we bought were right on! We found volumes on Watergate, the Making of Presidents, Subliminal Seduction, Double-Speak, and Automobile Safety.

About this time someone had an inspiration. They thought the American public might plunk down good money (not to be confused with the Susan B. Anthony dollar) for the opportunity to view an ancient Egyptian mummy and his artifacts on a whistle-stop tour of the United States.

They were right. We blew our budgets on boxcar loads of King Tut memorabilia. Actually, we did not blow our budgets, we simply fulfilled a need. Filling needs was important then.

We were asked to wear WIN buttons (Whip Inflation Now, remember?), about the time we were wondering just what it was that an ayatollah did for a living. We also started to seriously worry about our health. Some worried so much about losing their health and their youth that they started jogging. A surprising number are running against time to this very day. A regime of strenuous exercise must make one feel that life should be endured for an eternity.

In addition to being fit, having more money was not necessarily such a bad idea, either. Money wouldn't have to corrupt us; we could control it. Down-home values can go hand in hand with driving a BMW or a Volvo, and a personalized license plate ("2-ND IN" or "WITH IT") would show the world where our heads are really at.

We made a conscious decision to buy for our school libraries good books on Economics, Tennis, Running, Nutrition, and Skin Care, while books whose titles started with *The Inner Game of* ... or *The Joy of* ... could be found in our personal libraries.

No one was talking about the population bomb anymore, and since we were not getting any younger, many of us decided to hop to it and procreate while nobody was watching. During this lull in global awareness women who once preached the necessity of one-child families during their 20s, took fertility pills in their 40s.

Naturally, the added responsibilities of raising children made folks fret and stew over traditional values and the family unit. We started dressing for success, or was it for security? Conformity? Naw, we were still individuals, just like everyone else.

Oh, yes! We purchased some good materials for our Business, Home and Family Life, and Vocational Departments.

Then when Mount St. Helens blew, our volcano collections erupted. That area is currently experiencing a dormant phase.

And now that every middle-class family is required to have at least one gifted child, we see increases in Computer books and Literary Criticism collections, as well as a resurgence of the Classics.

Say, would anybody like to make a deal? I will trade two full boxes of books about Iron-Poor Blood, Hypoglycemia, and King Tut, for only five books on AIDS. How about Eating Disorders? Sex, Drugs, or Rock and Roll?

—L. A. P.

Technology Express
How to Merge into the Fast Lane

Technology. Everybody is talking about technology. Attend a meeting nowadays and all you hear is "cutting edge" this and "leading edge" that. It's enough to make one, well, edgy.

It is not that library media specialists are against technology; far from it! For years we have struggled to get basic technology like electric typewriters, telephones, and photoduplicating machines into our facilities. While many library media specialists might lust after security systems, the concept of computers that would print overdue notices, catalog cards, and keep track of circulation made us positively giddy. Then, seemingly overnight, our senses were deluged with a profusion of technological *stuff*. Before we could say "Melvil Dewey," we went from manually typing and filing catalog cards to networking on-line patron access stations. Why weren't we granted a few intermediary steps between our Stone Age and the Information Age?

Sometime in the future you will eventually decide (or someone will decide for you) that it is high time that your library tuned in, turned on, and dropped out from the old ways of doing things, to make contact with the exploding universe of information. This is foreign territory for most of us. You might get lost along the way. Then what will you do? What *will* you do? Do what those who have ventured upon these vast and mostly uncharted waters before you have done! Use the "Technology Express Program"! Don't go high tech without it.

1. Get hysterical. Go ahead, get it out of your system so you can enjoy the adrenaline rush of terror which will come later.

2. Learn what is out there. Attend all those workshops and conferences that you previously avoided. Get acquainted with the latest technological advances. Meetings held in major hotels are particularly attractive, because when you realize that there is simply far too much to learn in one lifetime, there should be a bar nearby. While your problem will not be soluble in alcohol, you may wish for anesthesia.

3. Ask around and find out what technology the library folks in your region are using. It is important that you visit these people. You will realize that they, like you, are in way over their heads. Bond with them. They will eventually be your support group.

4. Find an in-house expert to help you. Most districts have an evangelic "techie" or two running around. Nurture them. Not only will they help you locate which wires to connect and keys to press, but they are indispensable when things go wrong, and things can go seriously wrong. Techies also make excellent scapegoats. Teachers will blame you for trashing the old system when the newfangled one crashes, and since techies are a misunderstood minority who frequently have difficulty communicating to nontechies, the astute library media specialist will deflect all blame to the techie's poor guidance. This is no time for altruism. You will be out of your comfort zone and at your wit's end. A techie scapegoat can be your return ticket from emotional La-La Land.

5. Draft a proposal. Try not to look surprised when the administrator who balked at the purchase order for bookends will sign-off on a purchase order for an interactive video station and two computers with CD-ROM applications. More than likely he or she has no idea of what they will do, but administrative conferences have recently been ablaze with technological whistles and bells, which ultimately justify their existence.

6. Receive your order. The moment of truth comes when you first see the boxes filled with your technological wonders and realize that you are supposed to promote this stuff as you would a good book. Now is the time for that previously mentioned "adrenaline rush of terror." There will be so many manuals that you will not know which one to read first. That does not matter; they are all indecipherable. (Remember, the manuals were written by computer specialists, and as such, are unintelligible to the average college graduate.) After experiencing an anxiety attack or two, you will start to put your shipment together like a kindergartner—by looking at the pictures. Eventually, with the help of a few friends (see #3), it will magically work.

7. Show a few students, then stand back, and observe. They will teach you how it all operates.

—L. A. P.

The Computer Ball

"Who's your date for the Computer Ball?"

Tandy sighed. Leave it to Dyna to go straight for the jugular. "I don't think I'll be able to connect this year."

"Not connect?" Dyna could not believe her ears. "You've got to start networking! How do you expect to hook up with some dude if you keep yourself hidden in the school library?"

"I meet guys there," Tandy said halfheartedly.

"You call Hal a guy? That space cadet is so far out he's past the ozones. The modem hasn't even been invented that could access him. Listen, we've been deckmates since middle school. You have to admit that recently your social life has been erased."

Tandy was uncomfortable. She just could not compete with this new-generation Dyna. In the last few years Dyna's hardware had blossomed. It was just too darned easy for Dyna to attract guys. If Tandy didn't know better, she would have sworn that Dyna had discovered new and creative uses for silicone.

"Tandy! Get with the program! You're running a memory search again, aren't you? Face reality, chick. Your love life is scaled down."

"Dyna, you're full of BRS."

"Really?" Dyna looked at Tandy with sympathy. "Buddy, it's about time we re-established dialog."

"Was it that obvious?" thought Tandy. With a power surge of emotion, Tandy could see that Dyna was justified. Date times, always difficult to access, had lately been few and far between. As tears welled in her eyes, she hugged her old friend and blubbered, "Oh, what DOS I do NeXT?"

"Hey, all of us get our wires crossed now and again," Dyna soothed.

"Oh, how I wish I were a guy." Tandy said. "I could just go up to a girl and ask her out. Sometimes I even wish I could be that weird guy, Jo Wang, who goes up to every girl in the hall and asks for a date until someone finally agrees out of pity."

"What is this, Wang envy?" Dyna exclaimed. "Why don't I get Hewlett, my current mainframe, to set you up with a hot number? We could even do what our parents did. What did they call it? Tandem date? Series date? Parallel date? Something like that."

"Double date?" Tandy asked.

"Yeah, that's it!" Dyna giggled. "What outrageous terms they used in the old days. So what do you say? Shall we 'double date' the Computer Ball?"

"Well, I guess I'm critical. Might as well give it a try."

"All right!" Dyna squealed. "Now let's check our options. I know! How would you like to boot-up a first-rate program? I'm talkin' the quintessential dude. I'm talkin' Mr. Hard Disk Drive. I'm talkin' Vax-to-the-Max!"

"Who? Who?" Tandy couldn't wait.

"Honey, I'm talking about Chip Banks."

"Chip Banks?" was Tandy's sarcastic reply. "He's in love with Daisey Wheeler. "They're practically engaged."

"Byte your tongue, girl. They're not a number anymore. Chip batched and dumped her. He caught her in a top-down mode with an old boyfriend. It seems as though she couldn't sever her relationship with that old clone, Franklin, even though he is completely outdated."

"I don't know. What would he see in me? Besides, I think he is out of my league. Maybe I could get Hal."

"Ugh!" Dyna grunted.

"Fine. Okay, You win," Tandy sighed, "but just don't say anything to embarrass me."

In schools across America the morning promenade gives students a chance to circulate, to see who is going with whom, and to check out who is currently available. The promenade lets kids line up alliances and establish enemies. The promenade is cruising without cars.

Teachers think the promenade (if teachers think at all before the first bell) is little more than an obstacle course to navigate on the way to their rooms. The rare parent who stumbles onto this early morning ritual is usually intimidated by the gallons of hormones running rampant in the sons and daughters of the community and is subsequently aghast at the school for letting it happen.

It was on such a morning that Chip Banks strolled down the halls of Silicon Valley High, eyes downcast, feet shuffling. So deep in his funk was Chip that he did not notice that his friend, Hewlett, had been walking with him.

"Chip, you old hacker, what's shaking?" Hewlett tried to pierce his shell.

"Nothing," Chip replied. "Nothing at all, and my life is upside down, and I want to hide, or I just might run away, not that anyone would notice."

"Stop it!" Hewlett shouted as he grabbed Chip by the arm and gave it a tug. "You're turning in to a Boolean Operator. You can't go around feeling SCSI forever. Frankly, Daisey Wheeler just isn't worth it."

"You might be right, but I am the chairman of the Computer Ball committee, and I don't even have a date for it, not that I feel like going," Chip answered sadly.

"Trash that Boolean garbage right now! I mean it! Tell me, did you stop feeling sorry for yourself long enough to score a faculty chaperone?" Hewlett asked.

"Yeah. I got the keyboarding teaching, Dot Matrix," Chip mumbled.

"Chip, you've done so much work on this project that you've got to go. You even got that great new band, 'The LaserCats'!" Hewlett said. "Dyna and I have been talking, and we've come on-line with this great idea. Why don't you let us line up a girl for you, and we can go together?"

"Aw, I don't know."

"Come on, man," Hewlett coaxed. "You're in no frame of mind to cold-boot yourself a date."

"That's the truth. I'm not saying I'll do it, but whom did you have in mind?" Chip wondered.

"Dyna came up with this radical woman; a real cute little mother board. You might know her. She works in the library first period."

"Tandy?" Chip asked. "Look, she's real nice and all that, but I can't go with her."

"Why not?" asked a bewildered Hewlett. "Her baud rate's a perfect 10—a little slow, but a perfect copy, and real clean, if you know what I mean."

"I know, I know. But she has this thing about her that would just make it impossible for us to connect," Chip nervously answered.

"I don't get it. She's nice. She's cute. She's got great peripherals that are just begging to be digitized." As an afterthought, Hewlett added, "She's even smart."

"Hewlett, please don't torture me," Chip moaned. "As president of the Computer Club I just can't go out with her."

"Why not? She might have a fair response time."

Chip looked around to make sure nobody was listening, lowered his voice, and whispered, "She's into old technology. She's actually into books and reading. What a waste. What a terrible waste."

Hewlett gently placed a hand on Chip's shoulder, and said, "Chip, she needs someone to enlighten her. Who better than you to show Tandy the wonders of new and emerging technology? She doesn't know the miracle of CD-ROM, and probably hasn't even manipulated a joy stick."

"You really think so?" Chip ventured.

"Absolutely!" Hewlett assured. It was looking as though Chip was caving in, and that would make Dyna very happy, very happy indeed. "Actually, a lot of guys fantasize about opportunities like this."

"I don't know...." Chip hesitated.

"Dyna says that Tandy thinks you're good-looking," Hewlett hastily added, afraid the fish might slip the hook.

"Well, perhaps. Let me store it and play it back a few times," Chip said.

"After the Computer Ball we'll go to the View Point in my car, that is if you two are as compatible as I think you'll be. Heck, she'll probably interface on the first date. Something tells me that she's user friendly. I bet in no time at all you'll be experimenting with connectivity!"

"Oh, all right. If you can set it up, I'll go. I may not have the best time, and I'm sure she won't want to kiss me, especially in your car with you two in the front seat. I don't even know her handshake protocol! But just in case, I'm not going to eat any onions between now and then!" Chip laughed.

As Chip whistled his way down the hall he did not even see Daisey Wheeler holding hands with Franklin. And Daisey noticed him not noticing. And she was hurt. And Daisey wondered why she couldn't adjust to new programs, and she missed Chip terribly.

And that is the way it is at Silicon Valley High.

—L. A. P.

Weeding

Weeding a book collection is such a dirty, nasty job. It is also a risky activity, and not the sort of thing we highlight on our résumés.

We conceal, even from our families, the fact that we sometimes give books the old heave-ho. Who could telephone their mothers and say, "Guess what, Mom? Today I trashed 27 worthless books in the 500s!"

So why do we do it? We do it because (1) it has to be done and (2) we cannot delegate it.

We also weed our collections because five of our seven books on communism are written by J. Edgar Hoover; only two out of our 12 copies of *Ivanhoe* have circulated in the past decade; there is a limit to the number of times a book can be repaired; six volumes are missing from a 12-year-old set of encyclopedias; most of our books about the moon were written before Apollo 11; salmon swimming upstream to spawn is an illustration used to explain human sexuality; and your predecessor had the bright idea of cataloging all of those textbooks publishers have sent to be reviewed.

We weed because wonderful, vibrant, exciting books are obscured by all the deadwood.

Library media specialists swear sacred oaths to weed collections, but seldom do they start. Consider the obstacles!

- Pull the books

- Pull the catalog cards

- Pull the shelf-list cards

- Take the books off the inventory

- Purge your electronic records (where applicable)

- Remove all of the school's markings

- Stamp "Discarded—Do Not Return" on the books

- Store the books

- Get rid of the books

We need to be surreptitious in our weeding habits; this is the one time when we should avoid student and staff interaction. However, even the most clandestine among us will eventually get caught weeding. Then there is hell to pay.

The clever library media specialist has lain awake nights considering what he or she will say to those who stumble upon us tossing books.

"Whatever are you going to do with these wonderful books?" screeches the teacher who once taught *Ivanhoe.*

We could try the honest approach and hope to educate her. "I am weeding volumes that are dated, damaged, and overly duplicated. Our core collection is inadequate, and I will show the administration that our book budget desperately requires increased funding to meet today's needs."

What she learns is that you plan to toss her beloved *Ivanhoe* into the incinerator. "What kind of a librarian are you?" she hisses. "I thought librarians were supposed to love books, not *burn* them!"

Another method is to evade the issue by not volunteering the truth.

"These shelves are so crowded and dusty. It's time I did a little cleaning."

Will she buy it? Probably not. She has been teaching since *Ivanhoe* was a best-seller, and has experienced every lame trick imaginable. "So what do you plan to do with all these books, hmmm?"

Now you must either tell the dreadful truth, in which case you lose all credibility, or you might elect to stretch the truth a wee bit.

"I am making room for a new shipment of books. We will temporarily consign a few copies to storage."

This might work. However, she may wish to see the books in storage, or notice that we did not receive *that* many new books.

What should we do? What options are there?

Well, there is the bold-faced lie.

Every library media specialist believes in Honesty and Truth. No pens, chalk, or paper clips from school can be found in *our* homes. *We* would never conceal undocumented income from chaperoning, officiating, or tutoring. Of course not!

But this is serious stuff we are dealing with. Remember, taxpayers paid for those books. Do we truthfully want the taxpayers, or even our administrators, aware that we are getting rid of books? Heavens, we are putting our conference trips on the line!

Ethics be damned! There is much to be said for the bold-faced lie.

Library media specialists would do well to have a lie ready for every occasion. For instance, for the teacher of *Ivanhoe,* "They just don't write books like this anymore, do they? I think I'll have these rebound so that they may bring joy to the next generation."

What if she notices that the books do not return? You can tell her that the bindery or the shipping company lost them, and you'll certainly not do business with those folks again. Or you might blame it on computer error. "I understand the school's computer lost track of the bindery shipments." With a disgusted shake of the head, "You know how computers are." While this is an admittedly weak lie, people are likely to accept anything a computer does.

A student queries, "Are you throwing away all these books? Can I have them?"

Old library media specialists know that books that are given away always return to haunt them. Besides, parents will see the books at home and ask questions, and parents ask tough questions. So assume the demeanor of a lecturing teacher and say, "Johnny, you know there are certain areas in this great country of ours where children are less fortunate than you. These books are being donated to start a new library where ..." The kid will immediately turn you out and leave the premises.

Administrators can be tricky. Like police, they are never there when you need them but are always snooping around when you don't. Avoid answering their direct questions. Put the onus back on them by twisting their questions around so that they feel they are actually expected to do something. Administrators are not thrilled with hands-on activities.

When an administrator sneaks in, points to your book cart, and asks what you intend to do with the books, you bubble over with enthusiasm and reply, "What a pleasure to see you here! It's so refreshing to see an administrator take such an avid interest in books. I am thinking of organizing a 'read-in' where teachers and administrators model oral reading skills to our students." They love it when you talk like this. "Here, take this copy of *Ivanhoe* and choose a section. You will participate, won't you?"

The administrator will surely compliment your idea but will also go to great lengths to avoid performing. If your administrator volunteers to read a selection of his or her own choosing, you may safely tell the truth. That person will understand.

The custodian must also be considered. With the possible exception of the secretary, custodians are the only people who actually know what is going on in your school. Horror stories exist of custodians who have returned boxes of soiled books "rescued" from garbage dumps. Take them into your confidence. Find out what makes your custodians tick, then wind their clocks. They may even help you.

"Psst! John! If a six-pack of 'old Stubbly' mysteriously materialized in the attic, might all these boxes of books vanish up there?"

"Don't think so. That is a mighty big batch of heavy books to vanish *up* into the attic. You know, I bet they could replace a half-rack of 'Moose Jaw' *down* in the tunnels, under the boiler room, where nobody ever ventures."

A few remarkable libraries never need weeding. These libraries experience a shocking rash of after-hours vandalism. Books just seem to drop from sight. It is bizarre how these books disappear one section at a time, never to return, with nobody noticing.

Nobody, that is, except for the library media specialist and the custodians. And they're pretty sure it's them little people what's doing it.

Ten Ways to Get Rid of Discarded Books

You may send your weeded books to a mission school up the Amazon. Eventually someone from your community will travel there, find your discards, and notify the hometown press that your district is supporting counterrevolutionaries with local tax dollars.

The following items may prolong the time your discards remain in the great beyond. With a little luck you will have moved on or be retired by the time the books hit the fan.

1. Abandoned well: This is an outstanding receptable for discarded books. If it happens to be on school property that is off-limits to the general public, so much the better.

2. Recycle: Recycling saves trees, and the discarded books return in the form of new books!

3. Do an Ollie North/Richard Nixon: Shredded books make nice mulch for the horticulture classes. They might even shred them for you. Do any of the students resemble Fawn Hall?

4. Orphanages, nursing homes, Salvation Army, etc.: You can always provide books for the truly needy. One thing that they will truly need is better reading material, but if this is your choice, make sure you remove all school markings or they will be back faster than the time it takes to receive a book through I.L.L.

5. Dumpsters: Again, remove all the school markings and pack them in boxes. You may choose to deposit one box per week in the school dumpster, or plan an exciting dumping holiday in the big city, daylight hours only.

6. Book sale: Sales bring in revenue, but they are a lot of work for the money generated. Remember that you are trying to sell to students books that they wouldn't even try to steal. Parents may wonder why you would want to get rid of these dear old classics. Risky.

7. Donate them to your local Friends of the Library: The Friends hold rummage sales that benefit the public library. Again, folks might wonder why the school is giving away perfectly good books. As always, remember to remove all the school's markings.

8. Hide them: School storage space is scarce. Secret storage space is nonexistent, but just in case, ask your favorite custodian.

9. Homecoming bonfire: Volunteer to start next year's homecoming bonfire while everyone is at the game.

10. Gift wrap: Christmas vacation is an ideal time to gift wrap your boxes of discarded books. Place them in the back of a pickup truck, and drive to the city. Park in an alley just off a busy downtown interesection. Lock the truck and walk around the block. When you return the books will be gone! What a fun and exciting way to start your holiday season! It is also not as dangerous as it sounds, as long as you just remember to remove all....

—L. A. P.

I had not been the librarian at an elementary school for more than three days when the fourth grade teacher whispered in my ear that the former librarian had thrown books away at the city dump! Furthermore, the teacher had discovered them on one of her weekly trips to the dump, had rescued them and brought them back!

Knowing that I would have to be much more cunning than my predecessor, I thought through a number of nefarious schemes for disposing of a big box of worn out tomes. The idea came to me one Friday as I passed a reservoir on my way to a one-room school out in the country where I went to give library service. The next Friday, I loaded the books up and, on my way to the country school, threw them into the reservoir.

Like all novice criminals, I had not counted on one critical factor: books float! For an hour, I had horrible visions of the fourth grade teacher spending Saturday at the lake!   —David V. Loertscher

PART 7 POTPOURRI

In compiling this book I gathered materials that demanded to be printed, but that also simply refused to be organized. A number of items would not fit into assigned subject areas, even with the use of word-prods.

Some items show how far the profession has come, while others reflect how much things have stayed the same. A few have historic value, some are inspirational, and a couple are included only because I happen to like them. I hope you like them, too.　　　　—L. A. P.

Short and Sweet
A Hodgepodge of Cartoons, Sayings and Slogans, Affirmations and Anathemas

WE BRAKE *FOR BOOKS*

BAN ROBIN HOOD
TOO MUCH SAXON VIOLENCE

HAVE YOU HUGGED YOUR LIBRARIAN TODAY?
IT'S LONG OVERDUE

LIBRARIANS ARE NOVEL LOVERS

DEWEY?
YOU BET WE DO!

Cataloger's motto:
"Don't drop your drawers."
—David Loertscher

157

HAPPY BOOKER

KEEP ON BOOKIN'

THERE IS SOMETHING
IN MY LIBRARY
TO OFFEND EVERYONE

SHOCK YOUR PARENTS
READ A BOOK

HAPPINESS IS HAVING YOUR OWN
LIBRARY CARD

If librarians ruled:

IF SCHOOL LIBRARIANS RULED THE WORLD,
READING WOULD BE A VARSITY SPORT.

LIBRARIES ARE
WONDERFUL

CONVENTIONS ARE SOMETHING
A LOT OF PEOPLE LEAVE BEHIND
WHEN THEY ATTEND ONE

PIG OUT ON BOOKS

TAKE ME TO
YOUR READER

READING, WILLING,
AND ABLE

IT'S NINE O'CLOCK
DO YOU KNOW WHERE
YOUR HOMEWORK IS?

SO MANY BOOKS
SO LITTLE TIME

LIBRARIANS ARE LOVABLE

LOVE A LIBRARIAN

Poems

It Happened One Friday
by Ruth Street

I arrived at my desk; it was seven forty-five.
In swarmed the kids like bees to a hive.
All day they buzzed round me with questions so varied,
Up, down, round and round, my beleaguered mind scurried.
"Who wrote *Lorna Doone*?" "Will you sign my green slip?
I hate to miss school, but my folks took a trip."
"I need some material on foreign relations."
"Do you have a book of familiar quotations?"
"I want to read *Smoky*, is it always out?"
"Will you kindly tell me what *Main Street*'s about?"
"What is a classic?" "May I borrow two pins?"
"Please tell us the time when the assembly begins."
"May I go to my locker?" "I want Mendel's laws."
"My topic's inflation—the effect and the cause."
"I talked with a teacher, that's why I am late."
"Just where do I look for a copyright date?"
"Will you find me a picture of an evergreen tree?"
"I need an example of a good simile."
"Must I pay for this book? The case was our pup;
Before I could grab it, he got it chewed up!"
"Can you find for me a favorite poem?"
"I'm writing a speech about school and the home."
"For the last book you checked me I'm grateful to you;
I thought it so good I made Mom read it too."
"Do you know the difference between sit and set?"
"I need Emily Post or some etiquette."
"We're having a party and want some new games."
"Bill Cody's checked out, do you have Jesse James?"
"Shakespeare is my topic, do you have him in here?"
"Just where is that play called *No More Frontier*?"
"Why can't we whisper? We're taking our lessons—
The UNO, its charter and sessions."
"Does chromium begin with a *c* or a *k*?"
"My assignment for Tuesday is on TVA."
"Who was that old king so renowned for his wealth?"
"Debaters we are and our question is health."
"I can't find Poticelli, though I hunt and I hunt."
"We're the program committee and need a good stunt."
"A diagram, please, of the lungs of a frog."
"Why can't I find verbs in the card catalog?"

"Sorry to disturb, didn't mean to talk loud,
Will you find me a picture of a cumulus cloud?"

Without lull or surcease—six hours endless stream,
I cudgeled my brain—tried hard not to scream.
When the hands on the clock said three thirty-one,
Pronto! they departed. I was left all alone.
The books scattered round me were a vast disarray.
I began to restore them Dewey Decimal way.
In walked a teacher, fatigued with much care;
Wearily she sighed as she dropped to a chair,
"It's so peaceful in here, quiet, orderly too—
But how do you stand it with nothing to do?"

— Reprinted with permission. *Wilson Library
Bulletin*, May 1947.

"It's so quiet and peaceful...."

The Machine Librarian

Classification is Vexation,
    Accessioning doth appal;
Let's check our brains and chuck the Books,
    Let Dooee do it all!

— *Public Libraries*, 1925

The Library Mother Goose

(Jingles for catalogers)

Filer, Filer, all the whiler,
How does your catalog grow?
    Typed cards here
    And guide cards there
And printed ones all in a row.

Top floor hot
Bottom floor cold
Middle floor temperate
    Five days old.
None like it hot
Some liked it cold
All were glad when the hot spell broke
    Five days old.

There was an old woman who lived in a shoe
She had many books, but knew not what to do:
"You sort them, arrange them, and list them
  on cards,
"And mark them all neatly, then shelve them
  by yards."

Classification is a vexation,
Subject heading is as bad,
    The rule for a. c.
    Puzzles me,
And departments drive me mad.

Little Miss Elsie
Sat by the L C
    Filing her cards away;
There came an exhibit
With crowds to the limit
And frightened Miss Elsie away.

Sing a song of seminar,
    A room full of chaff,
Four and twenty analyticals
    For one small monograph.
When the tray was opened
    The subject cards showed off,
Wasn't that a perfect feast
    To set before a prof?

—*Libraries*, January 1926

Two Saints in One Act
by Nina Napier

Fate struck as she climbed the stairs one day.
With an armful of books in her usual way;

And just as she was, without preparation,
She arrived at her heavenly destination.

It happened that day Saint Peter had gone
Into town to have his halo shone,

And to keep another important date,
So he'd left Saint Paul in charge of the gate.

Paul looked out and his face was grim,
No sinner was going to get past him;

And he said: "Well, why are you standing there?
Come here and fill out this questionnaire."

So she filled in her name, her address and age,
And the state of her soul on another page.

The number of sermons to which she had listened,
And "Yes" to the question: Was she christened?

And when she had carefully answered it all,
Humbly she handed it back to Paul.

Paul took the form with a scornful look,
And entered it up in a big black book,

And he went to the files of the living and dead,
And hunted and hunted, and finally said:

"Well just as I thought, it's perfectly clear
You were never expected to turn up here;

And besides," he shouted, "if it comes to that,
You can't come in here without a hat!"

She picked up her books and turned to go,
When along came Saint Peter, all aglow,

Looked through the gate, and gave a shout:
"What are those books you're carrying about?"

And over his face came a wistful look,
"It's such a long time since I read a new book."

"Oh Sir," she said, "I'm sorry indeed,
I haven't a thing a saint would read,

Nothing to suit your taste in the least,
Not a single book by pope or priest."

"Hm," said Peter, "that's not what I mean,
Have you anything new by Ellery Queen?"

"Oh yes," she replied, and the saint with a grin,
Opened wide his gate, and said: "Come right in,

The Lord will welcome you into glory,
He's very fond of a mystery story."

"I see," he said, with a kind expression,
"You're a cataloguer by profession;

Librarians, I fear, to sin are prone,
So few have approached the golden throne.

But now, as a sign you've attained perfection,
I'll show you the Lord's own book collection;

How happy He'll be, how satisfied,
When He's had it properly classified!"

So the good saint led her to marble halls,
Where millions of books lined the jasper walls.

"You needn't hurry the work," said he,
"Dear child, you have all of Eternity."

Eternity waited; she sighed and said: "Well,
No wonder librarians go to Hell."

— *Library Levity*, Dogwood Press

Take a Librarian to Lunch
by Pike Johnson, Jr.

Take a Librarian to lunch.
You know she deserves it.
Ascertain her favorite food,
Then find a place that serves it.

Seek out, too, an ambiance
That you are sure will suit her:
Some place that bans all little kids,
And where there's no computer.

Serve her with her favorite drink:
Champagne? Or something diet?
And make it clear that, at this meal,
There are no rules on quiet.

Ask her to tell you of her job:
Which books are circulating?
Which patron said what funny thing?
You'll find it fascinating.

But do leave promptly when you've shared
Good talk and drink and food.
Librarians must be back when due
And may not be renewed.*

*Nothing here should be construed as precluding the taking of a male librarian to lunch.

— Reprinted with permission of
Connecticut Libraries.

Little Lyrics for Librarians
by William Fitch Smyth, 1910

A Librarian's Life is the Life for Me!

A librarian's life is the life for me

For there's nothing to do all day
you see,

but to sit at a desk and read
new books,

And admire yourself, and think
of your looks.

To questioning souls one can tartly
say:

"I can't be bothered with you
today,

For I haven't finished this novel.
See?"

A librarian's life is the life for me.

— Contributed by Patricia
L. Schmidgall

Popular View of Library Work
by Florence M. Hopkins, 1926

It must be a whole lot of fun

To be a trained librarian.

The only thing she has to do

Is just to read a good book through.

If someone wants a reference,

She turns her whirling chair just once,

Then takes a step or two about,

And sweetly says, "The book is out."

You're a WHAT!

by Carlene M. Aborn

Introductions are over, names have been exchanged,

A pause, a lull before job titles are interchanged.

"I'm a doctor," he proudly states.

"And I'm an attorney," she boldly relates.

"As for me," quips the next, "I'm a politician.

And this here gal, she's a fine mathematician."

And so it goes, all occupations clearly understood

Until it's my turn to state my livelihood.

With a smile on my face designed to captivate,

I quietly say, "I'm a media specialist," and then I wait.

Their eyes reflect the question, conversation ceases to be.

I remain silent and alert, aware of their perplexity.

Finally it comes, like a wheel spinning out of a rut,

Charging, dashing across the room — "You're a WHAT?"

"A media specialist," I repeat in a quiet voice.

"And it's a rewarding job of my very own choice."

"Oh, then you must be in television, that's an exciting career."

"No, I imagine it's advertising," spouts a voice from the rear.

"Perhaps she's in some sort of communications,

Or maybe even—the field of public relations."

The guesses go on, but still no one can say,

Just what a media specialist does for her pay.

I'm tiring of the game, my smile is wearing thin.

"I'm in library—audiovisual education," I shout above the din.

Again the sudden stillness, the disbelief I can always sense.

Their chagrin is apparent as they emerge from the suspense.

"You mean you're a mere librarian in some ordinary school."

And thus arrives that point when it's difficult to keep my cool.

Explaining the complex role of a media specialist requires skill,

For all too often, educational jargon creates waves of ill-will.

But even after explanations are through and you think they
comprehend your job—

Some character confronts you with a remark that makes you
want to sob!

"With a title like that," he says, "I'm certain you'll do fine,

In outwitting all of the panelists on 'What's My Line?'"

Owed to an Aide
by Dick Knudson

While I was sitting at home one night
With lots of time to kill,
I thought of all the aides I'd had—
Especially Elmer Hill;
Of how he'd struggled long and hard
Those tall tasks to fulfill;
Of how he'd stamped and checked in books
And delivered an overdue bill.
Yes, I pictured that lad all tuckered out
From the rind of the "library mill,"
And I grimaced, "There's nothing I
Can do to ease his pain" ... until—
Such an idea struck my brain,
I leaped up and sang, "I will!"

And so I hurried out last night
While stories were open still,
And bought this little present
For good old Elmer Hill.

Good Old Elmer Hill

At Christmas Time all hearts are warm
And hearth fires fry our "gills."
One needs a little something to
Combat the heat, I feel;
To give us rest from diligence,
Keep us from taking ill.
Therefore I purchased something
To act as a "cure-all" pill:
A triple-scoop ice cream cone—
It ought to fit the bill.
A triple-scoop ice cream cone
For good old Elmer Hill.

A Plea to the Children's Librarian
by Pike Johnson, Jr.

Don't computerize your catalogue.
Don't tamper with each tray.
Don't let the spindles dwindle.
Don't cart the cards away.

I know that, with computers,
Subject search becomes a game
At which five-year-olds are expert
And four-year-olds the same.

But I can't calmly contemplate
The tumult in the town
When the kids commence complaining
That the catalogue is down.

So don't let the labels languish.
Don't tell the tabs they're through.
What was good enough for Dewey
Should be good enough for you.

—Reprinted with permission of *Connecticut Libraries.*

From the Library
by Pike Johnson, Jr.

Our annual report

To the heads of the Town:

Circulation is up.

Computer is down.

—Reprinted with permission
of *Connecticut Libraries.*

School Librarian's Desiderata

Go placidly amid the shelves and carrels,
and remember what peace there was in reading rooms.

As far as possible without surrender be on good terms with all students. Speak your truth quietly and clearly; and listen to others, even the travelling sales rep.; they too have their story. Avoid loud and aggressive coordinators; they are distractions in the discussion rooms.

If you compare yourself with school board consultants you may become vain and bitter; for always there will be greater and lesser persons than yourself.

Record your procedures in your staff manual, as well as your plans. Keep interested in your own career, however humble. You at least know you're getting results.

Exercise caution in your selections; for information media are full of ambiguity. But let this not blind you to what innovation there is; many librarians strive for high loan statistics; and everywhere the resource center is full of learning experiences.

Be yourself. Especially, do not feign interest. Neither be cynical about teachers' cooperation; for in the face of all aridity and disenchantment it is perennial as the untidy shelves.

Don't drop your bundle. Today's disaster is tomorrow's workroom joke. Do not distress yourself with the cataloguing back-log. Much can be accomplished in the vacation.

Beyond an occasional evaluation of educational objectives, be gentle with yourself. You are a teacher, no less than the bursar or the caretaker; you have a right to be here. And whether or not it is clear to you, no doubt your program is unfolding as it should.

Therefore be at peace with the principal, whatever you conceive Him/Her to be; and whatever your labors and aspirations, in the noisy confusion of the circulation desk keep peace with your aide. With all its sham, drudgery and broken dreams it can still be a satisfying job. Be careful. Strive to be happy.

—As found posted to the workroom wall in an Australian school
library circa 1973, by C. Naslund. © 1986 Dyad Services.
Reprinted with permission from *Emergency Librarian*,
Department 284, Box C34069, Seattle, WA 98124-1069.

Stories and Essays

A Touch of Nostalgia
by Eric Garland

I guess I had never been quite so desperate for an eighth-period activity. I wouldn't have believed it, but there we were, a friend of mine and I, tromping through the tunnel toward the Lower School library.

"All of my favorite books are here," she told me, quite seriously. I scoffed then, although I would soon find that many of my own favorites were tucked away there as well.

"Can I help the two of you to find anything?" I had never met this librarian before, but she spoke warmly to me, like an old friend. She didn't ask me to leave when I opened my mouth nor did she slap me with a D-hall. Something was wrong. I felt silly just being in this youngsters' haven at first, then even more awkward on hands and knees searching for my own childhood "classics." I realized I had not felt so childish (or so *good*) in a long time. Crouched on the bright carpet amidst a pile of Beverly Cleary books, I became painfully aware of the child in me—largely ignored these days.

Thinking back now, I find it incredibly unfortunate that in the past few years, my intense desire to GROW UP AND BE BIG has completely overshadowed all of the wonders of being a kid. I read books just as often now as I did then (I used to write them as well), but today's fiction is somehow not as vivid, not as real. Perhaps even that sentiment seems corny and immature, but, then again, would I have cared as a second grader?

—*The Review* (St. John's School newspaper), Houston, Texas

Discipline in the Library

by Robert Gabrio

I was in the library when O. C., better known on campus as "Oh Sh-t" because of his constant discipline problems, came wandering into the library with a teacher's chalkboard pointer-stick. He was using the stick as a white cane, pretending to be blind, and causing such a disruption that my neck muscles tightened into knots before I could get a grip on myself. "Oh sh-t!" I thought to myself, and I sucked air!

Instead of immediately going through the usual exorcism, I waited until I was breathing a bit closer to normal, and then asked O. C. if I could see his stick. He was suspicious, but handed it to me, claiming that the stick was his since a teacher had given it to him.

I look closely at the stick, and then I asked him to look at it as well. He did so, and then he looked back at me a bit bewildered.

"Can't you see that?" I asked.

"What?" he responded.

"It says here you have to have a title to own this stick!" O. C. was sure I had gone crazy, and he told me so. We decided to have the librarian look at the stick.

She had evidently overheard our conversation. She studied the stick, then matter-of-factly stated, "It says here that you have to have a title to own this stick."

Now O. C. was losing his cool. I looked him straight in the eye and shrugged helplessly. "What can I say, O. C.? Do you have your title?"

He stared back at me, and for once *his* eyes silently said, "Oh sh-t!"

"You are all nuts!" was all he could say.

"How about we show this to Mr. Beckstead (the vice-principal) and let him see what is on this stick?" I asked.

O. C. was immediately in favor of this; he loves Mr. Beckstead—they hang around together quite a bit. He was certain good old Mr. B. would verify the fact that nothing was written on this stick.

Into the office we went. When Mr. Beckstead saw O. C., he quietly sighed, "Oh sh-t!" He looked at me, I winked, and he caught on that something was up. I explained that, as I read the fine print, this stick needed a title to verify ownership. O. C.'s mouth began to open, but the vice-principal's mouth was faster. He looked closely at the stick, and without missing a beat, said, "Not only is Mr. Gabrio right about the title, O. C., but just look at these license tabs—they are out of date!"

O. C.'s neck stiffened and *he* sucked air. I left feeling great!

Postscript: O.C. no longer causes disciplinary problems in my vicinity. He actually avoids me. I try to hide when I see him in the halls or else he goes the other way.

Networking in the West

by Ginny Vogel

Once upon a time, in a western state, there was a great deal of concern that librarians who worked with and served young adults were not getting together. It so happened that onto the scene came an energetic coordinator of young adult services for a major county library system who wanted to rectify the situation. She found another cohort in the city public library system and together they encouraged, cajoled, and actually browbeat librarians into attending the state conference of the school library group.

So over the mountains the public librarians tripped, many with apprehension that this was not the best use of their time.

Well, the first day went well, everyone was pleasant, but stayed in their own comfortable groups. The school people looked at the public librarians as some sort of strange but nice species, and the public library folks thought that school people when they are let loose go crazy.

Day two dawned and promised to be more of the same until ... dinner!!! What could have totally ended any hope of networking turned into one of those rare moments in history that people are still talking about. After a pleasant cocktail hour we all went to dinner. The conversation was lively until The Speaker. Memory has long since repressed the name of the speaker, and that is just as well. The lights dimmed, the introductions were done, and the speaker started. This may have been the most boring, most uninteresting speaker who has ever put an audience to sleep.

Fortunately, because of that cocktail hour beforehand, several people had a need to leave the room, and after taking care of that which caused them to leave the room, found themselves in the hallway reluctant to reenter the dining room. So they talked. They found that unattended bar and helped themselves. They giggled and soon they began to dance. What they did not realize was that through the glass on the doors everyone but the speaker could see this group of public and school librarians doing the cancan, right out there in the hallway, and having a lot more fun than the group inside. A few more folks came out and pretty soon the hall was filling up.

Well, the word soon got around that the school people really know how to have fun at conferences and more and more public librarians started coming and giving presentations and making friends and professional contacts.

That's how networking works in the West. A word of caution; this was not a scientifically designed and documented event. Replication may not be possible, but it is certainly worth a try.

The Indianola Academy Burglar Alarm
by Ellen Clayton

The story you are about to hear is true. Perhaps the names should be changed to protect the innocent (or not-so-innocent).

Last year a burglar alarm was installed at our elementary school library because of the theft of several VCRs, computers, and other valuable equipment. Apparently, that alarm was not sensitive or quick enough on the draw, for the thieves made off with two more VCRs before the police ever arrived at the scene. A new, more sensitive system was then installed. (Note the word *sensitive*; it will be important as the plot thickens.)

This November, during Children's Book Week, we had a wonderful contest featuring 26 book characters from A to Z. Colorful pictures of favorites starting with Amelia Bedelia and ending with a Dr. Seuss creature, Zizzer Zazzer Zuzz, were carefully taped to the library walls.

After a week of fun with our contest, at one o'clock on a Saturday morning, the library burglar alarm rang. The headmaster, Mr. Burns, was called out of a sound sleep, and he and the police surrounded the building. Then they waited, and *waited*—but the robbers never came out.

So ever so stealthily, with guns drawn, they entered the library. There, lying on the floor, was a poster of ol' Paul Bunyan eating a stack of pancakes. Obviously, this husky hero had fallen from the wall and set off that sensitive bell. And this, folks, believe it or not, is no TALL TALE!

Software Reflections

by Lawrence L. Jaffe

The computer software industry has entered the realm of our personal lives as well as education. Advertisements for these intriguing packages are interspersed between such traditional educational products as "Shaping Up with Geometry" and "Plain Geometry Made Simple." One recent listing shows a disk called "Personal Analysis, a New You in 30 Days" (only $9.95!). With current acknowledgment of stress and burnout in education, an inexpensive therapeutic package like this one might be most useful. However, what do you do if you don't like the new you, or even worse, no one else does? Will the company offer you a recovery program for $200, or condemn you to slide down the razor blade of life as a most despicable character?

Perhaps you have seen the program called "Interlude II." Advertised as "A Bed of Roses— Interlude #136; Why did you bring me so *many* roses?... Just the petals darling ... cool, velvety, fragrant." "Interlude II" is booted in concert with moonlight, a flickering fireplace, a flask of wine, and assists in establishing a program (*sic*) for a romantic evening. Finally a convincing argument for the purchase of a surge suppressor and backup power supply!

We even have a program called "Housecall: The Computerized Home Medical Advisor." Now you can quickly find out why you've been feeling poorly since celebrating your 30th birthday. I wonder if it has diagnoses for maladies caused by video terminal radiation? If your diagnosis turns out wrong, you can always turn to the law assistant package and initiate a suit against your computer for malpractice, although you should not sue a computer unless you are terminal, or have really crashed. And, of course, you can always return to one of the psychological help programs to rid yourself of anxieties caused by your misdiagnosis and computer aggravation.

If all this fails, you can escape with one of the olde English classics such as "Romeo and Juliet." Me, I'm leaving on the next flight of "Flight Simulator II." Bye.

Funny Mail

Received by Lawrence L. Jaffe
at Lionville Junior High

The use of computerized mail merges has produced some interesting and entertaining mail for us in recent years. Many of the names, addresses, and enclosures are based on an analysis of magazine records which would normally be an appropriate response to a home rather than a school. Some are obvious errors in entering the data by a humanoid.

Here are some of our favorites:

Wrangler Sailcloth Slacks Your Best Slacks Buy!
Mr. L. Lionville Jr.
Do me a favor, Mr. Lionville....

Cycle
Mr. Lionville Jr H S
The favor of a reply is requested, Mr. S.

Mr. and Mrs. Lionville Lib

Mrs. Lionville Sch.

Double Your Million $ Sweepstakes
Lionville Jr HS LIB
ENGLISH DEPT
"This is to certify that Lionville now residing at English Dept. in the town
     of ..."

Dear H S Lionville Jr.
     "I'm writing to you because from the list I found your name on, I think
you may be a lot like me!... Since I can't talk to you, H S Lionville Jr,... "

One biological supply company sent a catalog to a Mr. R. Sh-thead!! Obviously, we have no teachers with this name.

One of my favorites concerns a prize notification that I received at my home
address. I live on Gravel Pike. The letter was mailed to "Grave Pit."

Murphy and Friends Come to School

School Law of Survival: If the principal is advancing toward you with the obvious intention of
     doing you some favor, hide.

Murphy's Law of Weeding: There is no such thing as a discarded book. Discards are only on
     extended loan to the great beyond and will eventually come back to the library of origin.

Dewey's Weeding Corollary: Discarded books are always returned with great fanfare.

Counseling Placement Principle: Counseling's idea of the perfect student library assistant is
     someone who has recently transferred from another school, is currently failing four classes,
     and will not shower after P.E.

Forbidden Fruit Formula: A "censored" book gathers no dust.

Everybody's Belief: Everyone who works in the library is a librarian.

"By Next Period" Principle: We work so much with the urgent that we neglect the important.

"Hall Pass" Principle: Educators waste so much time on the trivial because we understand it.

Typing's Rule of Selection: When two keys are simultaneously hit, the wrong key will print.

Peeved Patron Law: The amount of information to be found on a given subject is in inverse proportion to the patron's belief that a vast amount of information exists on that subject.

Deadwood's Law: There is always a reason why nobody uses it.

"Friend in Need" Principle: The worst disciplinary problem can become the librarian's best friend when a term paper is due by the end of the day.

Murphy's Law of Duplicating Machines: Copy machines will break down when the staff is busiest.

Faculty Meeting Fact: The longer the principal speaks, the lower the faculty meeting's productivity.

A.V. Skill Theory: A.V. expertise is acquired in direct proportion to the number of times the equipment malfunctions.

"Those Damned Kids" Corollary: Force it when it jams; replace it when it breaks; blame it on the students.

"Have-at-It" Rule: New equipment goes to the teacher who is likely to abuse it the most so that the warranty may still be in effect when it disintegrates.

Librarian's Lament: You can lead the boy to the *Readers' Guide*, but you can't make him use it.

Law of the Index: Students know that it is easier to skim 100 books than to use one index.

Manufacturer's Rule: Equipment on warranty must be shipped in its original packaging, thus negating the warranty.

Security System Syndrome: The more elaborate the security system, the more the students will try to circumvent it.

A.V. Lecture Law: Tell the students that there are 1,000 miles of coaxial cable in the building and they will believe you. Tell them not to touch a "live" wire, and someone will invariably grasp it.

Whistles and Bells Belief: Technological toys often pass for progress.

A.V. "Heal Thyself" Observation: Equipment that has not functioned for months can mysteriously and temporarily work when the repairman arrives.

"Why Me?" Rule: When a library media specialist is presenting to other library media specialists, the equipment will malfunction.

Computer Cop-Out: Make a mistake, blame the computer.

English Teacher's Comment: It is less complicated to perform brain surgery on yourself than to understand computer software manuals.

Principal's Complaint: Computers were invented by Murphy.

Law of the Reference Question: No two people will ask for the same information in the same way.

Law of Many Happy Returns: The lost book will return after its replacement has been purchased.

Potty Formula: The number of times you "gotta go" is a result of the distance from the library to the lavatory, added to the number of cups of coffee consumed.

Sticky Situation Law: Pressure-sensitive labels that come with catalog kits stick only to themselves.

Call Number Comment: The smaller the book, the longer the call number.

"Oops" Factor: One mistake will negate 10 accomplishments.

Software Dilemma: A company will come out with a new, updated, and totally different version only after the last one is finally understood.

Laws of Book Shipments:
1. No matter where you hide it, teachers will always find the new shipment of books before it has been processed.
2. Teachers will "borrow" the unprocessed new books regardless of the amount of pleading, threats, and promises to reserve.
3. One in four of these "borrowed" books will never be returned.
4. Library staff will be faulted for not keeping better track of books.

Superintendent's Law: "In conclusion" means half of the speech is yet to come.

Best Buy Law: No matter how long you shop for something, the librarian in a neighboring district will buy the same item cheaper. If the librarian is your friend, she will tell you; if she is not your friend, she will tell everyone else.

Library Bait and Switch: Entice them with magazines and pulp; sell them on literature and substance.

"Mutt and Jeff" Principle: If you are tall, the book you want is on the bottom shelf. If you are short, the book you want is on the top shelf.

Fairness Doctrine: Teachers who send four unannounced classes to the library to do 10-page reports on parasitic organisms in humans deserve every page they get.

Increased Circulation Practice: Require teachers to properly borrow their books.

Jobber's Law: The most needed book will be out of stock.

Responsibility Trip: Librarians were responsible for books. Media specialists were responsible for A.V. Library media specialists are responsible for everything, everywhere.

"Write-Off" Law: Students seldom return borrowed pens and pencils. Teachers never return borrowed pens and pencils.

Secretary's Law: The pen nearest the telephone seldom works.
Secretary's Corollary: When the pen works, there will be no paper.

Office Principle: Give the junk mail to the library and take the best magazines home for a few weeks.

S.I. Swimsuit Law: After the swimsuit issue of *Sports Illustrated* is confiscated from the coaches— who stole it from the custodians, who took it from the secretaries, who claimed it from the student, who heisted it from your mailbox—it will never be seen in its entirety again.

Las Vegas Conference Factor: Administrative talent, insights, and expertise are dedicated to the job, but brilliance is saved for travel budgets.

School Policy Law: When common sense fails, follow school policy.

Mediocrity Occlusion: In every organization there exists one person whose job is to squelch creativity and reward mediocrity.

Rule of the Committee: When conflict occurs, form a committee of the most vocal combatants. Eventually the committee meetings will become more important than the problems they were meant to solve.

School Reform Law: True school reform is always from the bottom up because nobody holding a royal flush will ever call for a new deal.

School Policy Factor: School policy needs no logic.

Extension Cord Need Factor: The screen and the power outlet will be on the same wall.

Everyone's Truth: The longer someone has to wait for a book, the more important that book becomes.

Law of the Lamp: A different lamp will be required for next year's projector.

New Test Theory: When the kids know the answers, change the questions.

Textbook Paradox: The textbook universally detested was once unanimously adopted.

World Book Postulate: There will always be at least one teacher whose idea of a library assignment is to have students copy from encyclopedias.

Law of the Fiscal Year: Some of this year's orders will be taken out of next year's budget. This demonstrates to administration that the library media specialist did not need the money allocated, and the following year's budget will be cut accordingly.

Law of Budget Reductions: When the district must cut 5 percent from the budget, the "books and materials" budget will be cut by 50 percent.

Cold-Sweat Law: Learning style theory does not apply in rooms that are either too hot or too cold.

Music Man Law: Library media specialists will not be able to keep extension cords, secure adapters, enforce copyright policies, hide cassettes, or locate equipment when the music teacher is on a mission.

"Lost Cause" Principle: In every school there is someone who will continually lose keys, gradebook, and other possessions.

Law of First Resistance: Any proposed change in school routine will immediately seem stupid and unworkable.

"Do Unto Others" Rule: Teachers who do not distribute their overdue notices are automatically placed at the bottom of waiting lists.

Priority Principle: When scores of students and teachers are viewing major news events as they unfold on a television in the library media center, a teacher will complain that his 12 students are distracted from a footnoting exercise, and will request that the television be turned off.

National Geographic Solution: If you can't give it away, donate it to the library.

Murphy's Law of the Gift Book: There is no such thing as a gift book.

First-to-Go Rule: The best books are stolen first.

Standard Belief/Lie: "I turned it in already!"

Lost-Book Lie: The more adamant a student is about having returned his overdue book, the greater the probability that the book is in the student's locker.

Our Moral Imperative: Librarians must always liberate stolen books from garage sales.

Twain's Truth: No book is so outstanding that it can't be ruined when read as a classroom assignment.

Fractured Contract Language Fact: Library media specialists provide teacher prep time because there are more teachers than library media specialists.

Cheaper Book Law: The most expensive book in the latest shipment is currently remaindered for $2.95 at the local bookstore.

Law of the Supply Budget: Immediately after being notified that the supply budget is exhausted, the last projection lamp will blow.

Pat's Law: Duplicate copies result when subscriptions are extended. If one tries to rectify the situation, all copies cease arriving.

Student Repair Method: When putting equipment back together, any piece that can be put in upside down or backwards, will be. After the equipment is reassembled, there will always be at least one spare part left behind.

Library "Big Bang" Theory: Only full bookcarts tip over.

Custodian's Summer Reading Program: One newspaper will continue to arrive throughout the summer.

Helen's Law: A sure way to curtail the popularity of a book is to have it rebound.

Periodical Imperative: The missing magazine is the one most urgently needed.

Law of Supply and Neglect: The book a teacher demands this year will be forgotten about next year.

—L. A. P.

Standards and Guidelines

National Educational Association Guidelines
1921

- All pupils in both elementary and secondary schools should have ready access to books to the end that they may be trained (a) to love to read that which is worth while; (b) to supplement their school studies by the use of books other than text-books; (c) to use reference books easily and effectively; (d) to use intelligently both the school library and the public library.

- Every secondary school should have a trained librarian, and every elementary school should have trained library service.

- Trained librarians should have the same status as teachers or heads of departments of equal training and experience.

- Every school that provides training for teachers should require a course in the use of books and libraries and a course on the best literature for children.

- Every state should provide for the supervision of school libraries and for the certification of school librarians.

- The school system that does not make liberal provision for training in the use of libraries fails to do its full duty in the way of revealing to all future citizens the opportunity to know and to use the resources of the public library as a means of education.

Standards and Curricula in School Librarianship
1927

The child no longer studies geography. He studies how the world travels; how it is sheltered, clothed, and fed. As an individual he may be presented with a "challenge"; as a member of a group he helps to work out a project. In either case he attacks his subject from the point of view of the investigator and the doer, not merely from that of the learner and memorizer. The class descends upon the school library individually, collectively, or thru a committee. The librarian and the teacher have been in conference and the former is ready. For each child there is a book suited to his particular age, interest, and ability as far as the experience and expert knowledge of the librarian make it possible. But this is not all. This same librarian goes about it to train the child in the methods of independent investigation. He learns how to take notes; how to judge the value of a book from its date; how to use convenient tools like indexes and card catalogs. And so whether the school functions under the platoon plan with regularly scheduled library hours, or under the Dalton plan with its trend towards individual instruction, the library is of the very warp and woof of its educational scheme. There must be a room set apart, and books, and a library teacher, someone who combines knowledge of books and library technique with sufficient knowledge of educational methods to make the library an integral part of the school's educational scheme and not an appendage or an extra-curricular activity.

—ALA Board of Education for Librarianship

Requirements That Should Not Be Made—If the School Library Is Open Full Time
A Handbook for Teacher-Librarians
1931

- *To do general clerical office work*

    The librarian's position is in no sense a clerical one.

    She should have assistance herself from pupils or other persons able to help in the clerical work of the library.

- *To take care of text books*

    These do not belong in the library equipment and the librarian's time should not be taken for their care and distribution.

- *To teach other subjects in the curriculum*

- *To do hall and playground duty*

    The librarian's task differs from that of the teachers in the school in that she is there to serve all the teachers and all the pupils, not a certain group of children assigned to her. In order that this service may be available to all, her presence in the library is required continually during school and also before and after school.

- *To permit the library to be used as a detention room or as a place to send pupils when a teacher is otherwise occupied.*

The Status of the School Librarian
Inducements for Improvement
by Mildred Frances Davis, 1931

At the present time, school librarians fail to measure up to the teacher's yardstick because they lack, first: inducements and opportunities for self-improvement. Last year, I sent out questionnaires to the outstanding high schools in the State of Michigan. Out of the thirty-five schools reporting, twenty-eight stated that their librarians were not given opportunities of any kind for self-improvement. Only seven school systems out of thirty-five offered inducements to librarians. It is interesting to compare the variation among these seven. One puts librarians on a teacher basis allowing $100 for a trip to Europe and $50 for attending summer school. The second grants $50 for summer school. The third merely allows time off for attending summer school. No mention was made as to whether salary would be continuous or not. The fourth offers three months sabbatical leave with full pay for study or travel—helpful only to those who have been in the system seven years. The fifth also offers three months sabbatical leave for study or travel, but is confined to Senior Assistants only with no mention of continued salary. The sixth gives $150 for obtaining a higher degree. When half enough credits are earned $75 is added to the salary. The last offers $75 for fifteen credit hours earned up to a Master's degree.

In comparison, then, teachers working on a ten month schedule not only have their summers free, but are actually paid for improving themselves. While librarians working on a twelve month basis not only lack financial rewards for improving self, but even lack time off plus loss of salary if such is undertaken. Obviously, such a deficiency prevents the profession from demanding and maintaining the highest qualifications. Efforts should be made to impress school executives with the need of inducing self-improvement for librarians, because, they, like teachers, improve not only themselves by so doing, but are of increased value to the system.

VACATIONS

Second, school librarians fail to measure up to the teacher's yardstick, because they lack the same vacations and do not receive additional salary for additional weeks of work done. Naturally, the nervous strain of school life is as hard on the librarian as on the teacher. To preserve the former's health and personality, it is essential that she should enjoy the same vacation periods. If it is desirable to have the school library open during the summer, a special librarian should be appointed. If the regular librarian is willing to work summers, she should receive additional salary for additional weeks of work done....

SALARIES COMPARED

Since the additional educational qualifications demanded of librarians have been pointed out, the returns made on their investment should be considered. The average teacher with a college degree has a beginning salary of $1400 in most systems. The usual annual increase for teachers is $100. In five years, the teacher is earning $1800 a year. The average librarian with college and library training has a beginning salary of $1500. However, her usual annual increase is only $50. In five years the librarian is earning just $1700. The teacher with a year's less training has not only evened salary accounts, but is $100 ahead. That is not all. The teacher's salary is computed on a ten month basis, while, in many cases, that of the librarian is calculated on a twelve month plan.

— *Wilson Bulletin*, November 1931

Hardnox University
School of Library and Information
Science Catalog: Nonacademic
Year, 1991-92
by Carol Hole
(Adaptations by Larry Parsons, with approval)*

FACULTY

Al. A. Standard, Dean, *Professor of Library Administration*

Bibb Lee O'Graphy, *Associate Professor of Reference*

T. Slipp, *Instructor in Circulation*

Mae Netry, *Professor of Cataloging*

E. Z. Book, *Assistant Professor in Children's Work*

Shel Flist, *Instructor in Cataloging and Acquisitions*

Gay Lord, *Professor in Circulation*

Perry O'Dickle, *Assistant Professor of Serials*

Moe Beel, *Professor of Outreach Work*

Jerry Atrics, *Instructor in Outreach Work*

T. Nage, *Associate Professor of Work with Young Adults*

Fay Retail, *Professor of Children's Work*

Lou Sprocked, *Instructor in Educational Media*

C. D. Rom, *Professor of Technology*

Hi Smith, *Instructor in Educational Media*

HARDNOX: A NEW CONCEPT
IN LIBRARY STUDIES

It has long been clear to intelligent practitioners of the library profession that the education offered in conventional library schools is inadequate to supply the professional knowledges and competencies needed by the modern librarian who must survive in the real world of library life as she is lived.

In other words: let's face it, folks, out on the firing line, the MLS doesn't cut it.

In an effort to provide in-service training and realistic preparation for new recruits to the profession, the Santa Fe Regional Library (FL) has established its own library school, staffed exclusively by battle-hardened veterans of real library staffs. The new school is the first in the nation to offer a program of study leading to the degree of MRLLS (Master of Real Life Library Science). All aspects of the program are coordinated toward the one goal of preparing the student to cope, so that, having survived our curriculum, *nothing* he encounters in public and school libraries will find him unprepared. Our official school song says it best: "I Never Promised You a Rose Garden."

Tuition and Fees

Students will be expected to take instructors out for beer on a regular basis. The addition of (a) steak or (b) lobster will be required for a grade of A. Students who prefer to receive a B may substitute chopped sirloin or shrimp creole. A grade of C will be given for hamburgers or pizza.

Students of opposite sex from their instructor may satisfy grade requirements in other ways (or same sex, at instructor's discretion), by arrangement with the instructor.

Like all aspects of our academic program, our fee structure is intended to confront students (if need be, harshly) with the realities of the modern political-social environment in which libraries function. In line with this policy, any student who can prove that he or she has succeeded in cheating on an exam without detection receives an automatic grade of A.

Buildings and Grounds

All classes will be held in real libraries. That is, in poorly planned, over-heated and/or air-conditioned (depending on season), crowded, uncomfortable rooms jammed with too many desks and crammed with piles of paper and books in flagrant disregard of fire codes.

Rooms are fitted with speakers, bells, and alarms to simulate real-life situations for the school library media specialists. Bells will go off at scheduled and irregular intervals. Announcements will be aired only when something important is being said. The fire alarm is the signal for school librarians to evacuate the building in an orderly fashion. They must turn off the lights, close the doors, and shut the windows. Failure to accomplish the above within 60 seconds will require the offenders to stay after class and clean the blackboards and erasers.

Hours

Classes meet eight to five on all weekdays, plus every fourth weekend. Those in the school library media track will start each day with "The Pledge of Allegiance." Vacations will be short. Students majoring in Circulation will be required to come in on holidays to empty the book drop.

Class Loads

All students will be assigned more work than they can possibly complete. Frequent homework is mandatory. In keeping with our policy of "real-life" library experience, whenever workloads are greatest, students will be regularly interrupted by instructors who will (a) ask permission to use the bathroom, (b) phone to complain for 20 minutes about a dirty book, (c) require the student to read and act upon a memo from the administration.

Curriculum

Students are required to take at least two courses in each subject area to ensure a well-rounded exposure to the perils of all aspects of the profession. As a further "real-life" experience, students will frequently be required to "pinch hit" for another student who has called in sick by taking his exams for him, although they have not taken the course. No excuses for failure in such exams will be accepted.

Sports

Hardnox U. makes up for its tough atmosphere and endears itself to students by its encouragement of sports. All students must elect at least two of the following sports:

Staff Lounge Cleaning Team

Inflammatory Gossip Squad (last year's state champs)

Christmas Party Drinking Team (upperclassmen only)

Grumbling and Bitching (intramural)

Orienteering Squad (conducts field meets in which students attempt to reach a bathroom with toilet paper)

Buck Passing Relays

Surreptitious Book Truck Removal

Hide the Rub-On Letters and Stencils Team

Staff Picnic Beeer Relays

Staff Meeting Backbenchers

CATALOG OF COURSES

Cataloging and Acquisitions Department

CAT 101   Basic Cataloging Skills:

Students will learn typewriter ribbon removal and basic typewriter repair, how to type with a sticking *e* key, use of whiteout in error concealment, and special exercises to reduce butt-spread from excessive sitting. Points will be awarded for thickest finger calluses from prolonged filing and ability to type while conversing and eating chocolate cake.

CAT 346   Advanced Cataloging:

In this course, students choose up sides. One side chants *AACR2* rule by rule. Opposite team replies with reasons why rule is (a) impossible to implement, (b) silly, or (c) too much work. Winning team will receive A. Losers will forfeit coffee break. For extra credit, students may invent their own cataloging rules. Points will be awarded for originality, pickyness, and total incomprehensibility to the average library user.

Prerequisite: CAT 101 or demonstrated ability to read *AACR2* without falling asleep.

CAT 347   Acquisitions for the Masochist:

Explores the hazards of packaging used by jobbers. Students learn to open rolled newspapers without shredding the paper, slit strapping tape without slitting fingers, creative disposal methods for styrofoam packing, and use of the pry bar. Special attention to the problem of the fierce staple. Weekly weight-lifting lab is required for students who cannot press over 200 lbs.

CAT 401   Computer Cataloging Programs:

Students will be shown computers and programs which negate the need to have taken the previous cataloging classes.

Prerequisite: CAT 346 and CAT 347

CAT 409   Order Slip Decipherment:

Advanced students will explore the realm of esoteric cryptography, including: tracking down owners of indecipherable initials, distinguishing writing from chicken tracks (school chickens are specially trained for this purpose), codebreaking, filing the illegible title, and many sophisticated ways to make those who submit order slips sorry they did.

Circulation Department

CIR 105   Fundamentals of Circulation 1 (Desk Work):

Course emphasizes development of saintly patience and a high tolerance for undeserved criticism. Role play of common desk situations covers: smiling while being yelled at and hearing the same lame excuses endlessly repeated, cursing patrons in a voice only fellow staff can hear, grace under pressure, understanding the mumbling patron, and making change. Phlegmatic temperament and a taste for bondage and discipline will greatly enhance chances of success in this course.

CIR 106   Fundamentals of Circulation (Office Work):

As preparation for attention to detail needed for success in the field, students will look for needles in haystacks, removing one straw at a time. Those whose attention wanders will be horse-whipped. Required term projects include: stamping 1,000,000 T-slips, reading 100 linear miles of shelves (all books are by authors surnamed Smith), and searching for 200 reserves which the instructor hides at random on wrong shelves. Psychiatrist in attendance at all times for students who freak out.

CIR 492   The Overdue Notice:

Advanced course for survivors of CIR 105-6. Students are enabled to experience the genuine overdue milieu by being locked in a small, inadequately lighted room, where they stare at a TV screen with a bad case of snow while simultaneously pounding their fingertips bloody on a board studded with nails. They will be forbidden to stand up or stretch for eight hours.

Note: Students with visual handicaps or claustrophobia may exempt this course with a medical excuse.

CIR 578   Seminar on Stack Creeps:

Graduate students only. Analyzes varieties of creeps, including: the mis-shelver of books, the sleeper (with and without snores) and how to wake him successfully, the surreptitious smoker, the tobacco spitter, the loudmouth, the whistler, and the oblivious mother with screaming infant. Mature students will be introduced to the peeper, the feeler, the obscene suggestion-maker, and the flasher. Ability to telephone cops* in under three seconds will be emphasized.

*School librarians must try to locate an administrator who is not out of the building.
Prerequisite: CIR 105-6 and/or Black Belt.

Library Administration Department

ADMI 206   The Library Secretary:

Dr. Pavlov, special instructor, will condition students to tolerate incessant ringing of telephone bells while typing 120 words per minute, error-free. Lecture sessions cover: time sheets and how to juggle them, faking the monthly statistics, and covering for the boss. Lab sessions in tracking develop ability to stalk, locate, and secure items as diverse as (a) Baker and Taylor invoices from 1958, (b) spare keys to Bookmobile, (c) current Demco catalog, and (d) staff member hiding in ladies' john.

ADMI 398   Elements of Library Bookkeeping:

Students in this course will be required to demonstrate ability to become intimate buddies with staff of Purchasing and Finance Departments (Business Department for those in the school library media track) using only a telephone.

Course covers: saying no to petty cash requests and making change for soda or candy machines, deciphering the budget printout, telling the boss and staff that there is no more money, covering up before the auditor comes, explaining to the auditor, and fundamentals of embezzlement. Students must know how to wield a pocket calculator in a crisis.

ADMI 601   Care and Feeding of the Politician:

Assistant Directors and above only. Seminar equips administrators to survive amid library and school boards, commissioners, city managers, and other wild beasts. Topics covered are: professional expertise as a weapon, using jargon to mislead, how to lie with statistics, flattery, advanced flattery, bootlicking, standing on principle, and resigning in protest. During lab sessions, students are parachuted into jungle teeming with jaguars, anacondas, and headhunters during the rainy season, armed only with a copy of the ALA standards. No inoculations against tropical diseases are provided. Survivors receive a grade of "pass." Failures are buried.

Prerequisite: Paid-up life insurance.

Reference Department

REF 101 The Reference Interview:

Exciting course for those who enjoy guessing games. In lab sessions, students play 20 questions. Student who is "it" is allowed to change the object he is thinking of without telling anybody. Winners are those who succeed in preventing entire class from guessing what they are thinking, before the library closes.

REF 295 Search and Destroy:

Instructors in this course are chosen for their ability to concoct fiendish questions, misleadingly asked, and containing a maximum number of tricks and traps, which are answered in no known reference book. Students work out with 40-lb. books while being timed with stopwatch. All answers on the final exam are unacceptable to the instructor, who changes the question at will. Pop quizzes daily.

Note: Students with hernias should not elect this course.

REF 415 Research:

Course emphasizes ability to extract information from a book in minimum time despite obstacles designed to increase challenge, such as: miniscule print, no table of contents, index designed to be understood by theoretical physicists only, typographical errors and downright lies in text, random placement of misleading illustrations, no pagination, and missing volumes. Students will enjoy attempting the above while telephone and school bells ring continuously.

REF 592 The Card Catalog:

Note: It is not recommended that reference students attempt to understand the card catalog. Reasons for its arrangement and entries are known only to Catalogers, who cherish it as a carefully guarded trade secret. If, despite this, students elect to pursue this branch of knowledge, instructors will reluctantly attempt to explain the rudiments.

Prerequisite: Completion of kindergarten or demonstrated knowledge of the alphabet.

Children's Department

CHI 101 Basic Child Psychology:

Covers essentials needed by school library media specialists and those specializing in children's work, including: wheedling, coaxing, pleading, threatening, and elementary intimidation. Special attention is paid to practical aspects: removing wee-wee from rugs, overawing the parent, basic busywork, turning a deaf ear, and fundamentals for first aid. Students must demonstrate ability to get 35 children (choice of terrified preschoolers or egregious sixth graders) to line up on signal.

CHI 245 Advanced Children's Work:

Investigates typical problems of the average children's department and school library: shutting up the problem parent, the snotty brat and how to put him down, making a child an offer he can't refuse, how to deny record-player privileges, and basic wrestling holds. Class exercises include getting a half-Nelson on a 160-lb. 14-year-old and ejecting him without slipping a disk, and preventing the child from "helping" you shelve books.

CHI 383 Reader's Advisor and the Child:

Students must demonstrate ability to speak at least one foreign language from the following group: (a) three-year-old, (b) teenage, (c) riddles, and (d) educationese. Exercises will include: finding the snake, shark, and dinosaur books while blindfolded, choosing three easy books about Indians in under three seconds, locating sex books by sound of snickering alone, and explaining insane homework assignments. Students will be expected to memorize all titles in at least 100 juvenile series, in sequence.

CHI 666 Programming:

Advanced graduate students only. Instruction in projector repair, basic distraction techniques, and riot control will enable the student to face a howling mob of preteens unarmed except for the magic words, "Once upon a time," without fear (or at least without showing fear). Ability to make 100 name tags in under 60 minutes and development of Command Presence are equally emphasized.

Prerequisites: Graduation from any recognized acting school or two years Broadway experience.

Outreach Department

OUT 102 Basic Bookmobiling:

Students use special traveling labs to learn emergency engine repair, defensive driving, map reading, diagnosis of common childhood diseases, and emergency survival techniques. Requires memorization of: Dewey numbers of 1,000 popular subjects, authors, and titles of all current best-sellers and the location of all public bathrooms in the county. Weightlifting lab required for students unable to bench-press 200 lbs.

OUT 207 Hoosegow Librarianship:

Fundamentals of Jail Library management. Includes unarmed combat, conducting the cell-sweep, training the trusty, retraining the trusty after recapture, getting guards to let you in, getting guards to let you out again, and what to do till the warden comes. Emphasis on problem solving by case study method, including classic case of librarian who gave inmate book on locksmithing. Students required to dress conservatively and carry no sharp objects on their persons.

Note: Strongly recommended for school librarians, especially those serving schools with in-house detention rooms.

OUT 272   Serving the Senior Citizen:

Emphasizes mastery of the soothing telephone voice and ability to listen for long periods to unintelligible reminiscences. Students learn symptoms of common geriatric ailments and how to second-guess patron preferences sight unseen. Grief therapists help students learn to deal with the bereavement process when patron dies right after his I.L.L. finally arrives. Lab sessions teach how to detect dirty books without opening them.

OUT 654   Scheduling:

Advanced seminar for those wishing to master the socioeconomic structure of the community. Detailed knowledge of geography, school bus schedules, literacy levels, rural grocery stores, and tough neighborhoods will be acquired by all students as they learn to balance staff fatigue, patron needs, and mechanical breakdown to produce schedules that satisfy nobody. Any schedule that causes a circulation drop will result in failure in the course.

Prerequisites: Juggling 26B or demonstrated psychic ability.

OUT 666   Library Services to the Functionally Illiterate:

This is a prerequisite for Library Services to the Illiterate, OUT 687, and Library Services to the Dead, OUT 689.

This seminar operates on the philosophy that no one is immune to library service if library service is defined as filling a socioeconomic lacuna in the community. Participants will develop innovative methods of library service without recourse to the printed word. Films, videotapes, videodiscs, records, body language, exercise, discussion groups, etc., will be examined. No discussion of cost of service delivery will be entertained.

Library Foundations Department

Note: Courses in this department are required of all students, regardless of major.

FOU 420   ACRONYMS:

Required course. Endorsed (among others) by ALA, AECT, AASL, SRRT, IFLA, SCOLE, and YASD. Motto: "You can't tell the players without a scorecard." Students memorize hundreds of arcane acronyms and initialisms. A paper is required which must use at least 30 library/education related acronyms. Papers will be read by a jury of library and school board members. Successful papers are those which completely baffle the jury.

FOU 456   Book Selection:

Students learn to make something from nothing as they strive to produce a balanced book collection despite obstacles provided by instructor, who constantly declares books out of print or out of stock, raises book prices, lowers book budget, and withdraws existing books. Final exam consists of oral confrontation between student and local pressure group outraged by dirty books bought by student. Students who capitulate under pressure are drummed out of ALA. Students who don't are burned at the stake.

FOU 457   Dealing with the Censor:

This course enables the student to smile and outwardly seem in control of his or her emotions while overriding the body's basic desire to strangle a self-appointed guardian of society. Students will be taught to spot the problem book and magazine (it will have pages and a cover). Students will also be taught how to play records and tapes in the reverse direction in order to spot a hidden message (the process for doing this to CDs is not available at press time). School librarians will be taught how to perform a special exorcism to rid themselves of censors who masquerade as administrators.

FOU 458   A.V. Selection—Hardware:

Students learn that A.V. hardware is purchased from vendors who provide the best hospitality rooms at conferences, or who will repair items without making the librarian feel stupid for describing a projection lens as "that round, glass thing-a-ma-bob at the business-end of the projector, connected to the plastic do-hickey which you turn to get the fuzzyness out of the picture." The class teaches the library media specialist to successfully bluff peers and patrons into believing that he or she knows how various machines operate. Actual hands-on experience is gained by fixing equipment fellow students and staff have broken. Students are required to construct and demonstrate a video or slide-tape show.

FOU 460   A.V. Selection—Software:

Students in the library media track view and discuss various mediums and develop individual software selection criteria, which chiefly consists of learning how to delegate the responsibility to teachers and administrators. Public librarians will create feasible rationales why R- and X-rated videos should be lent to minors, and why *Debby Does Dallas* is not acquired, regardless of the number of patron requests.

Note: Students who provide popcorn and sodas at screenings receive extra credit.

FOU 470   Computer Selection:

Computers are now used in all facets of library work. Students will learn to select computers by carefully considering the opinions of experts, viewing demonstrations, and studying pigeon entrails.

Note: Computer software selection dart boards will also be constructed.

FOU 220   Role of the School Library Media Specialist:

Students will learn how to provide information and services for everyone to do anything, for a schizophrenic institution—American education.

Note: Students who demonstrate a basic knowledge of magic and illusion will not be required to take this course.

FOU 206   The Librarian Image:

Teaches students to dress and behave in a way befitting the image of the traditional librarian. Lectures include: choosing the sensible shoe, hair buns and how to make them, choosing spectacles, controlling the bustline, and developing the repressive facial expression. Course emphasizes development of ability to say "shhh!" with sincerity.

Prerequisites: Students must present affidavits that they do not smoke, drink, or consort with the opposite sex, or any other sex.

Every course has been verified by a Practicing Librarian in the relevant field as being absolutely essential to survival. A Hardnox education is guaranteed to ensure success in librarianship.

Index to Contributors

Index to Subjects
and Memorable Phrases